Leader's Guide

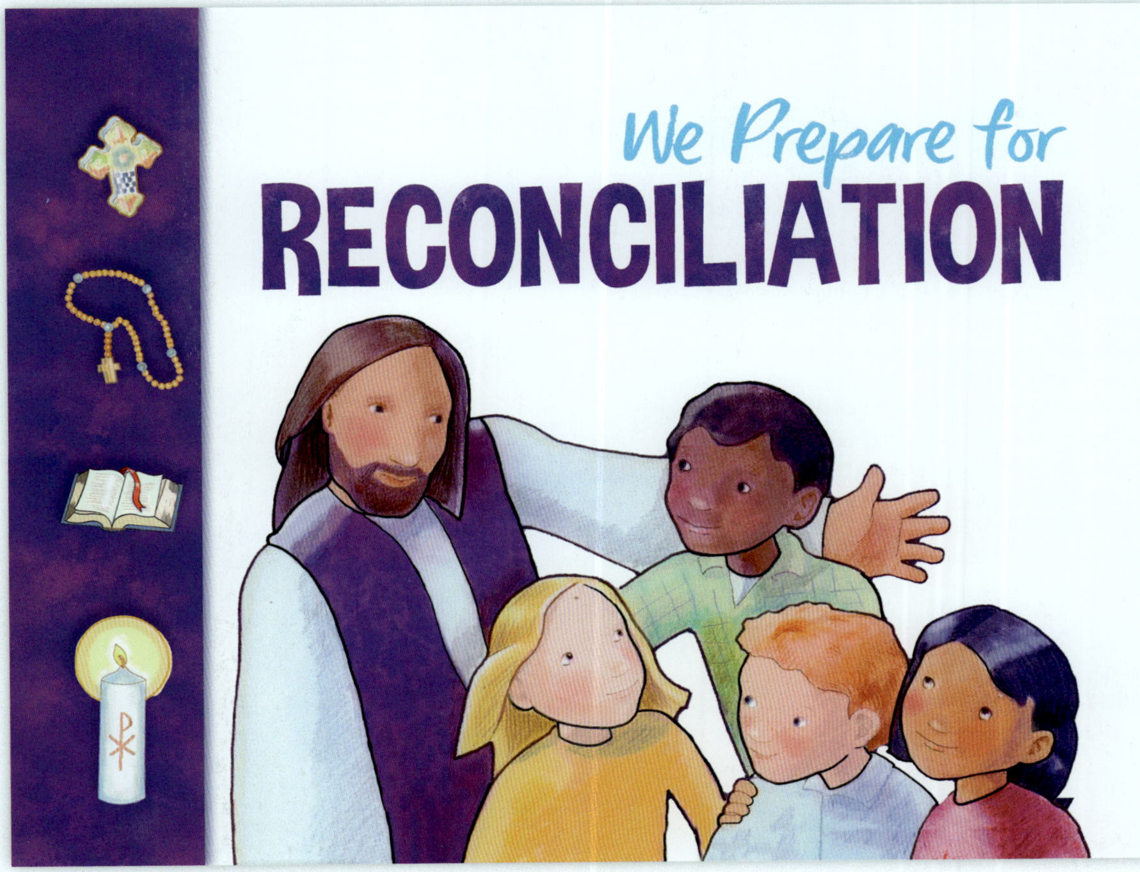

Authors
Françoise Darcy-Berube and Jean-Paul Berube

Editors
Gwen Costello and Myrtle Power

TWENTY-THIRD PUBLICATIONS

Sacramental Preparation Resources, 3rd edition
We Prepare for Reconciliation
We Share in the Eucharist

NOVALIS

Nihil Obstat
Caroline Altpeter IBVM
Archdiocese of Toronto
19 June 2009

Imprimatur
+Thomas Collins
Archbishop of Toronto
1 July 2009

Cover: Design: Celeste Gagnon; illustration: Anna Payne-Krzyzanowski

Design & Layout: Celeste Gagnon

Illustrations: Art Plus: pp. 4, 37, 39, 44, 47, 49, 51; Jocelyne Bouchard: p. 23; June Bradford: pp. 17, 24, 25, 27, 30, 31; Heather Collins: pp. 40, 41, 42, 43, 48; Suzanne Mogensen: pp. 6, 32, 33, 54, 55; Anna Payne-Krzyzanowski: pp. cover, 12, 13, 19, 20, 21, 29, 36, 46, 50, 52, and icons.

Photo credits: Page 3: © Jacek Chabraszewski/Dreamstime.com; Page 7: © WP Wittman Photography; Page 8: © Morgan Lane Photography/Shutterstock; Page 9: © iStockphoto.com/Carmen Martínez Banús; Page 10: © iStockphoto.com/Pathathai Chungyam; Page 11: © Felix Mizioznikov/Shutterstock; Page 14: bottom left: © iStockphoto.com/Leah-Anne Thompson; Page 14: top right: © iStockphoto.com/Özgür Donmaz; Page 14: bottom right: © iStockphoto.com/Yenwen Lu; Page 15: left: © iStockphoto.com/Rich Legg; Page 15: right: © iStockphoto.com/ Doug Schneider; Page 16: left: © WP Wittman Photography; Page 16: right: © Jacek Chabraszewski/Dreamstime.com; Page 18: © Marzanna Syncerz/Dreamstime.com; Page 22: 2009 © Geo Martinez. Image from BigStockPhoto.com; Page 26: © iStockphoto.com/ RonTech2000; Page 28: 2009 © Edward Mahala. Image from BigStockPhoto.com; Page 34: © Nic Neish/Shutterstock; Page 35: © R. Gino Santa Maria/Shutterstock; Page 38: 2009 © Cathy Yeulet. Image from BigStockPhoto.com; Page 39: © 2009 Jupiterimages Corporation/Goodshoot; Page 53: © iStockphoto.com/Juan Gabriel Estey; Page 56: © Monkey Business Images/Dreamstime.com

Publishing Office:
1 Eglinton Avenue East, Suite 800
Toronto, ON, Canada
M4P 3A1

Head Office:
4475 Frontenac Street
Montreal, QC, Canada
H2H 2S2

Tel: 416-363-3303 Toll-Free: 1-877-702-7773
Fax: 416-363-9409 Toll-Free: 1-877-702-7775
E-mail: resources@novalis.ca
www.novalis.ca
ISBN: 978-2-89688-671-5 (Novalis)

Cataloguing in Publication is available from Library and Archives Canada.

We acknowledge the support of the Government of Canada.

Published in the United States by
Twenty-Third Publications
A division of Bayard, Inc.
One Montauk Avenue, Suite 200
New London, CT 06320

www.twentythirdpublications.com

ISBN: 978-1-62785-455-9 (Twenty-Third Publications)
Library of Congress Control Number: 2019936389

Printed in Canada

Order extra activities for children free of charge at twentythirdpublications.com in the FREE E-Resources section.

MIX
Paper from responsible sources
FSC® C148846

Table of Contents

Welcome!

You are about to begin the journey of walking with parish children and their parents towards the sacrament of Reconciliation. Baptized children sometimes prepare for and celebrate Reconciliation before they complete full Christian initiation (that is, celebrate Confirmation and Eucharist). Reconciliation, however, is not a sacrament of initiation. The initiation sacraments are Baptism, Confirmation, and Eucharist.

In the early Church, most people who sought to become Christians were adults. They were baptized and confirmed before celebrating the Eucharist. Over the years, influenced by both theology and practice, these three sacraments were separated. Children were baptized as infants; later, usually at age seven, they were prepared for Reconciliation before celebrating First Communion. Church leaders still require that children at least learn about sin and Reconciliation before First Communion; in some parishes, children celebrate the sacrament of Reconciliation when they are older.

This book can be used in either situation, as it focuses on introducing children to a Christian way of life. It emphasizes the central place of Jesus in their lives and invites them into a prayerful relationship with God. It also emphasizes the virtues of love, joy, peace, and forgiveness, which pave the way for the sacrament. The final theme offers immediate preparation for the sacrament of Reconciliation.

We believe that you as a parish catechist, working with and walking with parents and their children, are immensely important as a guide and mentor in preparing children for their first experience of Reconciliation. Enjoy the journey, and as you walk it, may you too experience God's love, joy, peace, and forgiveness.

The Journey of Initiation

The *ongoing process* of entering into the mystery of Christ, which is discovered and experienced in the sacraments, is called Christian Initiation. We slowly and continuously grow "into" Christ throughout our lives. As we have already seen, the notion of initiation developed early on in the Church. This process for individuals and families took place in five clearly defined stages:

1. It had a precise beginning when the candidate's request to become a Christian was officially accepted.

2. The initiatory process began. During this stage, the candidate was taught how to live gospel values, learned about the Church's customs and traditions, and practised various forms of prayer.

3. When they were ready, the candidates celebrated Baptism and Confirmation, followed by participation in the Eucharistic meal.

4. The *mystagogy* period came next. At this time, the new Christian tried to deepen his or her experience of Christ by reflecting on all that had happened. (*Mystagogy* is from a Greek word that means "studying the mysteries" of our faith.)

5. At the end of the initiation journey, the person began a responsible Christian life.

Living a "Christian life" means living the way Jesus did. By looking at and listening to Jesus in the gospel stories, we and those we teach can gradually come to know him and his message better. A key aspect of this message is forgiveness. Other aspects include compassion for those who suffer; helping the poor, the sick, and the imprisoned; and sharing with those in need. Jesus challenges us to be light for the world through our words and actions. In this program, you will guide children in this process, introducing them to a lifelong practice of forgiving and being forgiven.

From the Bible

We are the children of God.
~ adapted from
1 John 3:1

Your Journey Begins

All around the world, thousands of boys and girls have begun this **journey**. They are hoping to find new life and to share God's love, joy, peace, and forgiveness. They, like you, are preparing to celebrate the **sacrament of Reconciliation** for the first time.

See how excited and happy they are. Where are you in this picture?

6

THEME: Your Journey Begins

FOCUS: **Children all over the world are journeying to find a new life and to share God's love, joy, peace, and forgiveness.**

GOAL **To assure the children that they are not alone as they prepare for First Reconciliation**

- Ask the children to study the picture on page 6. Who is pictured? Where do they fit in this scene? Invite them to put themselves in the picture.
- Ask why they think the children in the picture are so happy. Is meeting God a happy thing for them? Why or why not? How do the children in your class feel about meeting God in the sacrament of Reconciliation?
- Explain that God loves them as beloved "children." Read the Bible passage, then have the children repeat it after you three times. Explain that God has given all of us the gift of life. Other gifts from God are love, joy, peace, and forgiveness.

Did You Know?

Our Christian Virtues

Virtues are gifts from God. They can lead us to moral excellence. Personal virtues help us to work for individual and community well-being, and thus are "good" by definition. The opposite of virtue is vice. In the past, we have thought of virtues as burdens, not as gifts. We have seen them as deeds we must do. But virtues are spiritual gifts that enable us to relate to God and others better.

- Faith, hope, and love are known as the "theological virtues," because they help us grow closer to God. (The word "theology" means "the study of God.")
- The gifts and fruits of the Holy Spirit are virtues. They include peace, joy, patience, gentleness, forgiveness, wisdom, kindness, love, goodness, and more. In this program, we will focus on the gifts of love, joy, peace, and forgiveness, which help us draw closer to God and one another.

You were first invited to walk on the path to God when your parents presented you for **baptism**. You were probably very young then.

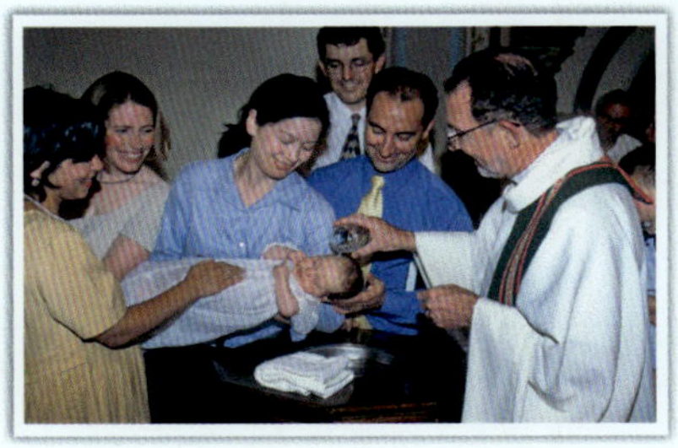

Now that you are older, you can understand better what baptism means. It means you belong to God's family. You are a member of the Church. You are a child of God.

The Church Teaches...

The sacrament of baptism is the first step on the journey of faith. Baptism points the way to God.
– adapted for children from Catechism of the Catholic Church (CCC) #1253

Words to Remember...

Journey – a special trip that you need to prepare for with care

Sacraments – seven great church celebrations in which Jesus touches our lives

Reconciliation – a sacrament that celebrates God's forgiveness in a special way

Baptism – the first sacrament, which joins us to the family of God and prepares us to celebrate the other sacraments, especially the Eucharist

7

FOCUS: **Baptism is the first sacrament of initiation.**

GOAL **To help the children understand that their journey of Christian initiation begins with Baptism**

- Invite the children to look at the picture. Explain that each of them was baptized when they were younger. Walk with them through these steps of the baptismal ritual:

— The priest or deacon welcomes the child, parents, and godparents.
— Parents and godparents make the Sign of the Cross on the child's forehead.
— Parents, godparents, and all present renew their baptismal promises.
— The baby is baptized.
— The priest or deacon anoints the baby with sacred oil.
— The child's candle is lit from the Paschal candle.
— All pray the Our Father.

- Go over the "Words to Remember" and explain each one. Be sure the children can describe them in their own words, or at least have some understanding of their meaning. Make a colourful wall chart of these words.
- Read the message "From the Bible" at the top of page 6. Ask each child to take a turn saying the words "I am a child of God" in a loud, clear voice while lifting up his or her arms.

1. God Gives You Life

Life is wonderful and amazing! To see its beauty, you must open wide your eyes and your heart. Life is a gift from God.

Look around you. See the sky and the sun. You may see flowers, animals, fish, and birds. You may see snowflakes. At nighttime, look at the moon and the stars. All of these are gifts from God.

Let us Pray

Here is a beautiful way to praise God. The Church has used this prayer for hundreds of years. When you say it, remember that you are praying with other believers all over the world. Say it often and try to remember it.

Glory to the Father,
and to the Son,
and to the Holy Spirit:
as it was in the beginning,
is now,
and will be forever.
Amen.

THEME: *God Gives You Life*

FOCUS: **How appropriate that Theme 1 begins with a prayer of praise to God for giving us life!**

GOAL **To help the children recognize God's gifts and to offer praise for them**

- Invite the children to discuss the picture on page 8. What are the children in the picture doing? Where do they seem to be? Have the children in front of you ever been in a similar place? What did they see and hear? Did they remember to thank God for the flowers, trees, fish, animals, birds, sky, and sun? Explain that all of these are gifts of life from God.
- Focus now on "Let us Pray." Read together the explanation of the prayer, then invite the children to pray it by repeating each line after you.
- Talk about the Father, the Son, and the Holy Spirit. These are three ways that we refer to God: as Father and Creator of us all; as Jesus Christ, Son of God, who teaches us the Christian way in the gospels; and as the Holy Spirit, who is with us always. The Church knows God as the Blessed Trinity. ("Trinity" comes from *trinitas*, a Latin word meaning "three.") Now pray the prayer again, with the children reading along with you.
- Ask the children if they know any other prayer to the Father, Son, and Spirit (Trinity). Remind them that the Sign of the Cross is such a prayer. Close by making this sign of our faith together. If some children in your group do not know how to make the Sign of the Cross, guide them as they learn it.

Life – how great it is! How beautiful! Through days and nights, through summer, fall, winter, and spring, God helps life to change and grow.

See if you can unscramble the sentence below:

NKTAH UOY DGO ROF EHT FGIT FO FELI!

____

Did you know? God asks YOU to care for the life that fills our world. What can you do today to care for God's gifts?

Today I can ______________________________

From the Bible

You have made me inside and out, O God. You watched over me in my mother's womb. I give you thanks that I am so wonderfully made.

~ adapted from Psalm 139:13-14

9

GOAL **To help the children understand that caring for life and our world is part of our Christian call to follow Jesus**

- Invite the children to look at the picture and share ideas about what is happening there.
- Read the words at the top left of the child's page, then have them work on unscrambling the sentence. Give them hints if they find this task difficult.
- Ask the children to close their eyes as you pray the "From the Bible" words. With their eyes still closed, they are to repeat the words after you. Invite them to share their thoughts about what this prayer means.
- Have the children fill in ways they care for the earth.

Did You Know?

Sins against the Earth

Caring for our planet Earth is an important Christian responsibility, but people did not always know it. Today, we recognize that humans are responsible for the damage that pollution and greenhouse gases are doing to the planet.

In 2008, the Vatican announced seven new deadly sins, including pollution, that are offensive to God. (The original seven deadly sins are pride, envy, gluttony, lust, anger, greed, and sloth.) The underlying attitudes for all seven new sins are the same—a lack of respect for others and for all of creation.

You Are Fully Alive!

It's amazing what you can do because you are alive. You can do things you don't even think about, like breathing, seeing, moving, and jumping.

Here are ways to think about how you are fully alive.

1. Sit down in a chair and put your hands on your lap. Close your eyes and take deep **breaths** three or four times. Then sit very still and listen to your heartbeat. Do you hear it?
2. Feel the air entering your body and giving it life. Then say out loud, "My voice, too, is a gift from God."
3. Smile a big smile and then open your eyes. Slowly stand up, raise your arms, and start moving them all around. Kick your feet up and down.

See all that you can do! Isn't it wonderful to be alive?

10

THEME: *You Are Fully Alive!*

FOCUS: **Life is a great gift, but we often take it for granted.**

GOAL **To help the children focus on the gift of life and all they are able to do because of it**

- Read the message at the top of page 10. Ask the children if they ever think about breathing, seeing, moving, and jumping.
- Look at the picture and invite the children to comment on it. How is the child using the gift of life?
- Slowly lead the children through the "awareness of life" exercise. Allow sufficient time for them to do each exercise. (When you get to number three, have them do this in silence if there are other classes nearby.)
- Have the children use the four lines on page 11 to write the things they do best.
- Read the Bible words on page 11 aloud, clearly and dramatically. Then have the children repeat these after you line by line.

Of all the things you can do because God has made you fully alive, which four things can you do best?

1. ______________________
2. ______________________
3. ______________________
4. ______________________

God made you the way you are. Here is what God says about you in the Bible:

From the Bible

You are beautiful in my eyes. I love you. I have called you by your name. You are my child!
~ adapted from Isaiah 45:4

11

Notes for Catechists

Show a Little Life!

Don't be afraid to be a "fool for Christ." In other words, when you are teaching about your faith, be dramatic, use exaggerated facial expressions, speak in a loud, clear voice, and use gestures. You want your message to reach eyes and ears, but also hearts! Encourage the children to role-play dramatically, to say prayer words enthusiastically, and to participate fully. Don't begin until you have everyone's attention. Never pray unless there is silence first. And don't be afraid to repeat and repeat until the children have grasped what you are saying and can repeat it back. Above all, have a sense of humour. Make religion class a fun place to learn about God, Jesus, and the Catholic faith.

Saint Francis loved life

Francis lived a very long time ago in Assisi, a little town in the country of Italy. Just like you, Francis wanted to be happy. His father was rich, so he had plenty of food to eat, nice clothes to wear, lots of toys and games to play with, and he had fun with his friends.

When he became a man, Francis knew that deep down in his heart, he was not really happy. One day he walked to an old church and sat down in the quiet space. He felt something tugging at his heart. He felt God speaking to him.

"Yes," Francis thought, "God is calling me to do something more with my life." From then on, he left behind his riches so he could follow Jesus. After that, everything he saw in God's creation filled him with happiness and joy. He cried out, "Praise to you, Lord, for our brother the sun and our sister the moon!"

12

THEME: Saint Francis loved life

FOCUS: **Francis of Assisi prayed with animals, birds, the sun, and the moon!**

GOAL **To introduce the children to a saint who obviously loved God and the gift of life**

- Ask the children if they have ever heard about or read about St. Francis. Have they ever been to a blessing of the animals?
- Read the first two paragraphs on page 12 and have the children look at the art.
- Invite the children to close their eyes and picture Francis in the old church. Everything was still and quiet there. That's when Francis heard God's voice deep within him.
- Ask the children if God has ever spoken to them. When? What did (does) God say to them? Share examples of times when you felt God speaking to you.
- Continue reading the story of St. Francis (last paragraph). Then explain that Francis chose to become a monk, someone who tries to pay attention to God and to help God's poor ones. Other men followed Francis in this way of life: they are known as Franciscans. They, too, want to be close to God and serve others.
- Now read the story of the wolf on page 13. Many stories like this were told about Francis. Although they may be exaggerated, they show his great love for all of God's creatures.
- Invite the children to close their eyes and imagine a little bird landing on their arm. What does it feel like? Is the bird singing or sitting quietly?
- Now share the "Let us Pray" on page 13. Read the prayer two lines at a time (loudly and dramatically) and encourage the children to shout out, "Thank you, God!" after each section. Then invite them to take turns reading the lines themselves, while the others continue to pray, "Thank you, God!"
- Ask the children which family members and friends they are particularly grateful for. Have them write these names on the lines at the bottom of the page.

One day, it is said, Francis even tamed a wild wolf. He said, "Brother wolf, please stop scaring the people. Go back to your forest. You will be happier there." The wolf did just as Francis asked. Little birds would sometimes land on his arm and sing God's praises with Francis. All the animals loved him.

Write here the names of some of your family members and friends.

____

____

____

____

____

____

____

Let us Pray

If you want to thank God as Francis did, you can say this prayer. When you get to the words "Thank you, God!" shout them out with joy.

For the sun that fills the sky,
for the moon and the stars at night,
Thank you, God!

For the wind in the trees,
for the rain that falls on the earth,
Thank you, God!

For the fish and the birds,
for the animals in the forest,
Thank you, God!

For my family and friends,
for my life and happiness,
Thank you, God!

13

Notes for Catechists

Shouting Our Praise!

Should we really "shout" when we pray? Should children? Here's how Psalm 47 says to pray ...

"Clap your hands, all you peoples;
shout to God with loud songs of joy."

Psalm 66 says something similar:
"Make a joyful noise to God, all the earth."

Prayer should at times be an experience of spontaneous joy. Encourage the children to pray to God often during their day in just this way.

A Prayer for You

May today you have peace within.
May you trust God that you are
exactly where you are meant to be.
May you not forget the infinite
possibilities that are born of faith.
May you use those gifts
that you have received,
and pass on the love that has
been given to you ...
May you be content knowing
you are a child of God.
Let God's presence settle into your bones,
and allow your soul the freedom to
sing, dance, praise, and love.
God is always there for you.
- attributed to St. Therese of Lisieux

From the Bible

Make others happy with the gifts God has given you.
~ adapted from 1 Peter 4:10

God Gives You Talents!

Do you know what it means to be **unique**? It means there is no one like you in the whole world – no one. God made you with your own smile, your own face, your own body. God gave you special gifts called **talents**. Your talents are the things you do very well.

There once was a boy named Henry. Many other children lived in his neighbourhood.

There was Momei, who could play the piano and sing.

There was Luis, who could kick a soccer ball farther than anyone.

There was Samuel, who always got the best marks in school.

There was Julie, who could run and jump higher than Henry could.

14

THEME: God Gives You Talents

FOCUS: **What a wonderful thing it is to be "unique in all the world."**

GOAL **To help the children be aware of and appreciate their gifts and talents, and, above all, their uniqueness**

- Read the first paragraph on page 14. Ask the children, "Does anyone smile exactly the way you do? Is any voice the same? Any face?" How do they explain their answers?
- Invite them to look at the photograph at the top right and describe what they see. What is the boy's talent (listening, being friendly, other)? What is the girl's talent (bottom right)? What is the other boy's talent (left)?
- Explain that the Catholic Church teaches that our talents are gifts from God. All gifts from God are meant to be used, and not just stored away out of sight.
- The Bible teaches us how to use our talents. Invite the children to read "From the Bible" together.
- Now share the first two questions from "Something to Think About" on page 15. Allow the children sufficient time to share. When all have had a turn, read the rest of page 14.
- Invite the children to comment on these talents and on the pictures.
- Now read the three paragraphs on page 15. What do they think of Henry's talent? Had they ever thought of being a friend as a talent? What does it take to be a good friend? End by praying together, "Thank you, Jesus, for my special talent."
- Review the "Words to Remember" on page 15. Be sure that the children can describe the terms in their own words. (Add them to your chart of "Words to Remember," if you have made one.)

At first, Henry was jealous of all these talents. Then one day his mother said, "Henry, you are always so kind to everyone. You are a very good friend."

Henry understood that being a good friend was his special talent.

At bedtime he prayed, "Thank you, Jesus, for my special talent."

Something to Think About

- What is your special talent?
- What other talents do you have?
- Are you a good friend like Henry?
- Do you thank God every day for your talents?

The Church Teaches...

Our talents are God's gifts.
- adapted from CCC #2009

Words to Remember...

Breath ~ a gift from God that helps you be fully alive

Praise ~ a way to tell God and others how wonderful they are

Unique ~ one of a kind in all the world

Talents ~ the things you do very well

15

Notes for Catechists

What's the Purpose?

Why does a book about First Reconciliation focus on life as a gift and on talents and uniqueness? There is a good reason. For children to grasp the concepts of conscience and reconciliation, they must first understand that they are responsible for their words, thoughts, and actions, especially in their relationships with others. If they value these relationships, they will try to develop their gifts and talents and use them in positive ways. To be the best they can be, they must be responsible and attentive. They must recognize God's gifts and use them wisely. When the text discusses sin a little later, they will better see it as a misuse of their gifts and talents. This will help them to be more open to reconciliation—with God and others.

You Can Talk to God

As you can see, God loves you very much. When you spend time talking to God, you are loving God back. Talking to God is called **prayer**.

Ask your family to help you set up a space in your room or home where you can go to pray. You can call this your "prayer corner." Make it special and beautiful.

In this space, put colourful pictures, a Bible, and anything else that reminds you of God.

In the morning, say, "Good morning, God."
In the evening, say, "Good night, God."

All day long, you can speak to God about whatever you are doing.

You can say, "Dear God, you are great. Thanks so much for all you do."

When you spend time each day talking with God and saying thanks, you will have joy in your heart.

16

THEME: *You Can Talk to God*

FOCUS: **"Loving God back" is a great definition of prayer!**

GOAL **To help the children feel comfortable with prayer as talking to God**

- Ask the children about the pictures on page 16. Is this the way they pray? Do they ver sit still at home, close their eyes, and talk to God? If not, why not? Where do they pray?
- Read the first two paragraphs aloud. Then take plenty of time to discuss how the children might choose a space for prayer: their very own "prayer corner." Explain that this can be a tiny space in their room or elsewhere at home where they can sit, close their eyes, and pray. Ask if they have a Bible at home or pictures or other things that remind them of God, such as items found in nature. If they do not, give each child a piece of blank paper. Have him or her write on it "My Prayer Corner" and decorate the page. They can use this sign to mark the spot at home they will use for prayer.
- The suggestions for prayer in the third paragraph can be used in the children's prayer corners. Practise them together by having the children repeat each line after you. Ask what other prayers they can use. This is a good time to review the Sign of the Cross and the Glory to God (the Gloria).
- Emphasize the sentence in the gold oval. Ask the children to share their definitions of "joy in your heart."

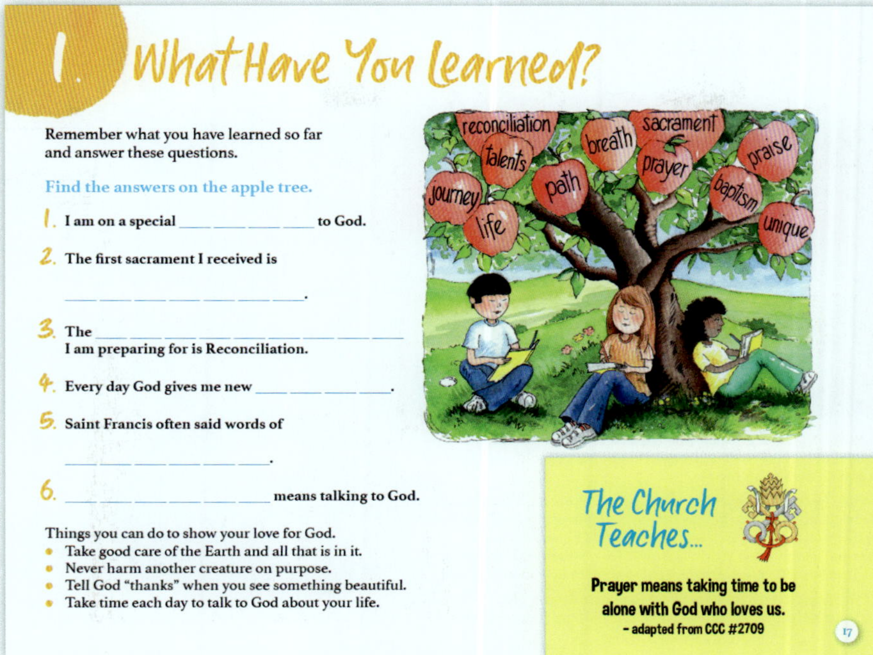

1. What Have You Learned?

Remember what you have learned so far
and answer these questions.

Find the answers on the apple tree.

1. I am on a special __________ to God.
2. The first sacrament I received is __________.
3. The __________ I am preparing for is Reconciliation.
4. Every day God gives me new __________.
5. Saint Francis often said words of __________.
6. __________ means talking to God.

Things you can do to show your love for God.

- Take good care of the Earth and all that is in it.
- Never harm another creature on purpose.
- Tell God "thanks" when you see something beautiful.
- Take time each day to talk to God about your life.

The Church Teaches...

Prayer means taking time to be alone with God who loves us.
- adapted from CCC #2709

17

THEME: What Have You Learned?

FOCUS: God's Gift of Life

GOAL **To help the children review and discuss what they have learned so far**

- Read through the six phrases one by one. Give the children time to look for the answers on the apple tree. Remind them to count the letters and find a word with that number of letters. As they find each word, invite them to move to the next one. When all have found the words, say each sentence aloud and have them repeat it after you.
- Review the things children can do to show their love for God, including caring for the Earth, animals and other creatures, and people. Invite the children to illustrate one of the four actions for their prayer corner.
- Before you close, read the Church's teaching on the meaning of prayer and have the children repeat it after you. Pray together the prayer on page 13.

A Prayer for You

Lord Jesus, you are challenging me
to unlock the truth of your Word
for and with those I teach.
But first I need to unlock it within myself,
to open the eyes of my own heart,
that I might truly and deeply know you.
Please turn the rusty key of my
faith and understanding,
that I might recognize you once again,
as if for the first time.
I do long to know who you are.
I do long to share your presence with those I teach.
May I proclaim your Word so fully,
and be so strong in my convictions,
that their hearts, too, will open,
and together we can pray ...
"You are the Christ, the Son of the
Living God, both now and forever.
Amen."

2. God Gives You Love

Jesus is the best teacher when it comes to love. Even as a child he studied the Word of God. He learned about the **Law of Love** that God gave to the Jewish people.

While he was growing up, Jesus tried to follow God's Law of Love. Little by little, he found the way to true happiness. It is NOT through riches, or power, or beauty, or being famous. The way to true happiness, Jesus found, is through great love. Jesus spoke about God's love with the people and he showed them how to love others.

If you want to be happy, look for God's love in your life. Open your heart to sharing, forgiving, and helping those in need.

Sit quietly and think about these words. Ask Jesus to help you understand them deep within your heart.

"You shall love the Lord your God with all your heart, and with all your soul, and with all your might, and your neighbour as yourself."

~ adapted from Deuteronomy 6:5 and Mark 12:31

From the Bible

Now faith, hope and love abide, these three; and the greatest of these is love.

~ 1 Corinthians 13:13

18

THEME: God Gives You Love

FOCUS: **God's Law of Love is a joy and never a burden!**

GOAL **To help the children understand that happiness comes from loving God and others; Jesus gives us an example to follow**

- Explain that we use the word "love" every day, but what does it really mean to love someone? Invite the children's input. Is love easy? Is it easy to love everyone?
- Then ask: Who can teach us how to love? After they offer answers, read page 18. What did Jesus learn? What did he teach others? How did he show love for God and others?
- Read the Bible words aloud, then have the children say them. Devise a "chant" they can repeat after you. For example: We have Faith! *(they repeat)* We have Hope! *(they repeat)* We have Love! *(they repeat)* We have these three! *(they repeat)* The greatest of these is Love! *(they repeat)*
- Now share how God defines love, reading aloud to them God's Law of Love from Scripture. If possible, make copies of this passage. Invite the children to decorate the page and place it in their prayer corner at home.

A Happy Celebration

One day Jesus came to a town called Capernaum. The people ran to greet him because they had heard about his preaching and healing. Jesus was happy to meet them and tell them about God's love. But the day was hot and in the evening Jesus was very tired. Many sick people were still waiting to see him.

When he saw this, he felt sorry for them. He forgot how tired he was. He took time with each one, blessing them and healing them all.

Imagine the celebration that evening in Capernaum!

Something to Think About

- Why didn't Jesus tell the people, "Come back tomorrow. I'm too tired right now"?
- What would you have done when you saw all those people?
- What do you do now when you are tired but someone needs your help?

19

THEME: *A Happy Celebration*

FOCUS: **Love means giving to others even when we don't feel like it!**

GOAL **To give the children an example of the meaning of love and of how Jesus offered love to those around him**

- Read aloud the three paragraphs on page 19, then have the children focus on the picture. What do they see? Ask them to repeat, in their own words, what happened.
- Go through the "Something to Think About" questions one by one. Invite the children to share examples from the third question. How did they feel when they helped someone?
- Tell the children you would like to share with them the healing blessing of Jesus. Invite each child to come forward one at a time. Place your hands on his or her head as you pray, "May Jesus bless you and heal you." Each child answers, "Amen."

Did You Know?

Healing in the Gospels

Jesus healed many people from disease or disability. Here are some examples:

- **Fever:** Jesus healed Simon Peter's mother-in-law. When other people heard about it, they came to Jesus for healing, too.
- **Long-term bleeding:** When a woman who had been bleeding for twelve years touched Jesus' cloak, she was instantly healed.
- **Blindness:** Jesus met a blind beggar who identified Jesus as the Jewish Messiah. Jesus gave the man back his sight.
- **Paralysis:** Jesus was in a house teaching when a paralyzed man was lowered through the roof because a crowd blocked the door. Jesus told the man to pick up his mat and walk, and he did!

Jesus often said, "Your sins are forgiven." Every part of the person, including the body, is made whole.

A Story of Love and Forgiveness

One of Jesus' best friends was Peter. He was a fisherman who worked hard to take care of his family. One day Jesus said to him, "Why don't you change jobs? Come and be my helper." Peter liked that idea.

He put down his fishing nets and went with Jesus. He listened and he learned about God's Law of Love.

The Church Teaches...

Be merciful and forgiving, as Jesus was, and love others as he has loved us.
- adapted for children from CCC #2842

"Love one another as I have loved you." This is what Jesus asks us to do.

20

THEME: A Story of Love and Forgiveness

FOCUS: True love always includes forgiveness.

GOAL To introduce the children to Peter and his need for forgiveness

- Ask the children if they have ever heard of St. Peter. What do they remember about him? Explain that he was one of the twelve people Jesus picked to be apostles (special followers). Then read the story on page 20.
- Peter was happy to follow Jesus when things were going well, but when Jesus was arrested, Peter was afraid. Ask the children if they have ever been afraid and yet did something brave. Invite them to share their experiences. Then ask if they have ever been so afraid, they couldn't be brave.
- Explain that even if we are not brave, Jesus is with us and forgives us. Read the words on the bottom right of page 20. Then have the children repeat them after you five times.
- Focus on the illustrations on pages 20 and 21. Invite the children to describe them.

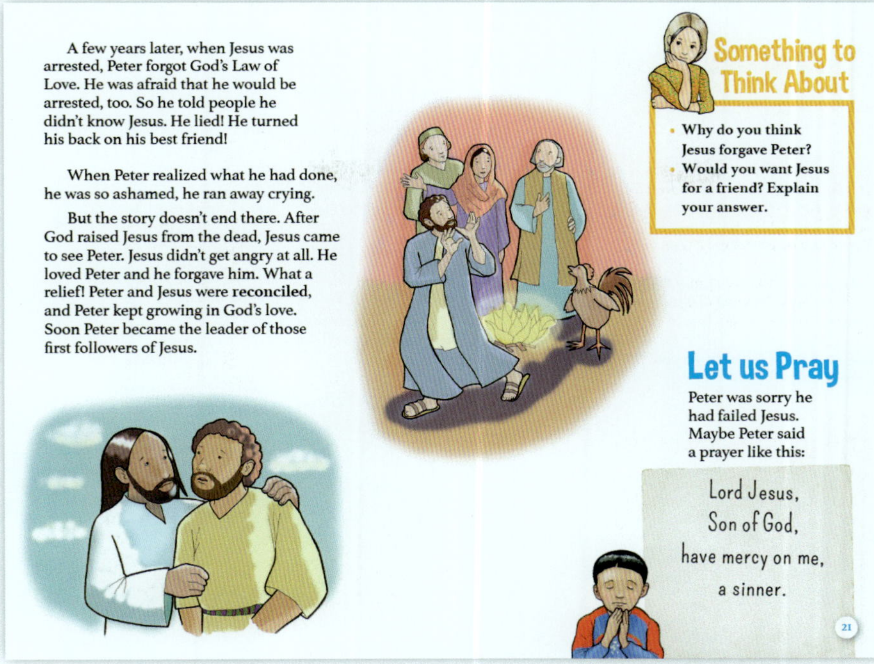

A few years later, when Jesus was arrested, Peter forgot God's Law of Love. He was afraid that he would be arrested, too. So he told people he didn't know Jesus. He lied! He turned his back on his best friend!

When Peter realized what he had done, he was so ashamed, he ran away crying.

But the story doesn't end there. After God raised Jesus from the dead, Jesus came to see Peter. Jesus didn't get angry at all. He loved Peter and he forgave him. What a relief! Peter and Jesus were **reconciled**, and Peter kept growing in God's love. Soon Peter became the leader of those first followers of Jesus.

Something to Think About

- Why do you think Jesus forgave Peter?
- Would you want Jesus for a friend? Explain your answer.

Let us Pray

Peter was sorry he had failed Jesus. Maybe Peter said a prayer like this:

Lord Jesus,
Son of God,
have mercy on me,
a sinner.

21

- Read the rest of the story (on page 21). Then read "Something to Think About" on page 21. Allow time for the children to share their responses.
- Share what the Church teaches about love and forgiveness. Invite the children to read this section silently, then ask for volunteers to read it slowly and dramatically. Explain that the Church has a special book that contains all its teachings. This book is called the *Catechism of the Catholic Church*. The teaching on page 20 comes from that book.
- Now look at "Let us Pray" on page 21. Invite the children to repeat it after you, then read it aloud together.

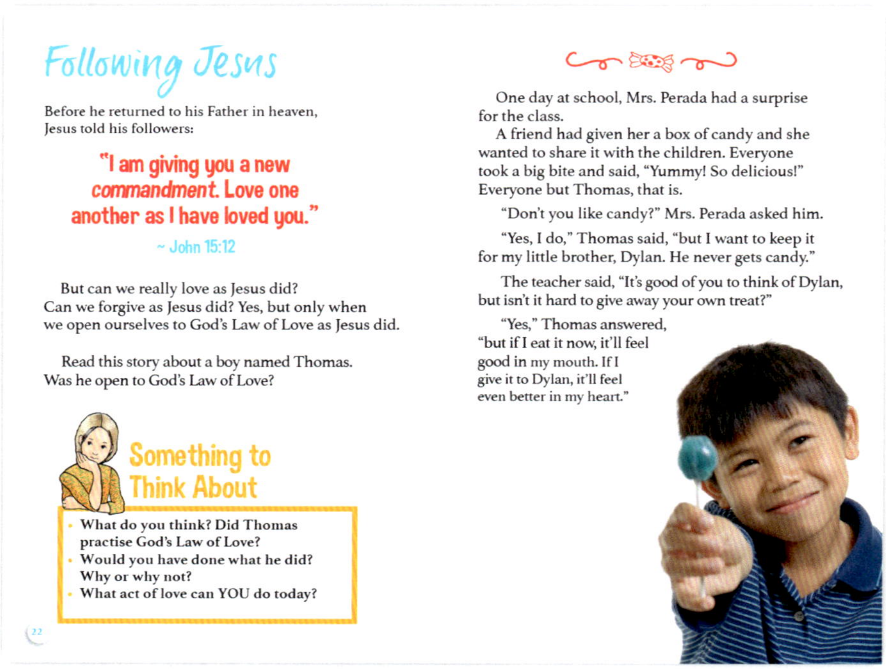

Following Jesus

Before he returned to his Father in heaven, Jesus told his followers:

"I am giving you a new commandment. Love one another as I have loved you."
~ John 15:12

But can we really love as Jesus did? Can we forgive as Jesus did? Yes, but only when we open ourselves to God's Law of Love as Jesus did.

Read this story about a boy named Thomas. Was he open to God's Law of Love?

Something to Think About

- What do you think? Did Thomas practise God's Law of Love?
- Would you have done what he did? Why or why not?
- What act of love can YOU do today?

One day at school, Mrs. Perada had a surprise for the class.

A friend had given her a box of candy and she wanted to share it with the children. Everyone took a big bite and said, "Yummy! So delicious!" Everyone but Thomas, that is.

"Don't you like candy?" Mrs. Perada asked him.

"Yes, I do," Thomas said, "but I want to keep it for my little brother, Dylan. He never gets candy."

The teacher said, "It's good of you to think of Dylan, but isn't it hard to give away your own treat?"

"Yes," Thomas answered, "but if I eat it now, it'll feel good in my mouth. If I give it to Dylan, it'll feel even better in my heart."

22

THEME: Following Jesus

FOCUS: To be like Jesus is to be loving and forgiving.

GOAL To share with the children Jesus' greatest commandment

- Explain that there are many commandments (rules for living) in the Bible, but here (in column 1, in red) Jesus gives us a new commandment that is greater than all the others. It might sound easy, but it takes courage and daily effort.
- Have the children take turns reading the story on page 22.
- Now invite them to role-play the scenario, taking turns as the teacher, the class, and Thomas.
- Go over the "Something to Think About" questions one by one. Does anyone remember "God's Law of Love"? (see page 18).
- Invite the children to write out or illustrate one act of love they can do this week. They can add these pages to their prayer corner at home.

Notes for Catechists

The Way of Jesus

Jesus taught his followers a "way" or path. He saw each person's religious life as a journey. He talked about seeking and entering the kingdom or reign of God. These are active words. They imply doing something, moving from where we are to someplace new. Jesus called people to follow him as a way of living. That is why the earliest members of the Jesus movement were known as "followers of the Way." It is to this vision that the voice of Jesus calls us today. His call to "Come, follow me" still rings out 20 centuries after his death. His life, teachings, and actions were focused on creating a new kind of personal and community life amidst the old one. Jesus set out to transform human life and to challenge the forces that oppress and divide people in every society. This is the journey he invites us to join.

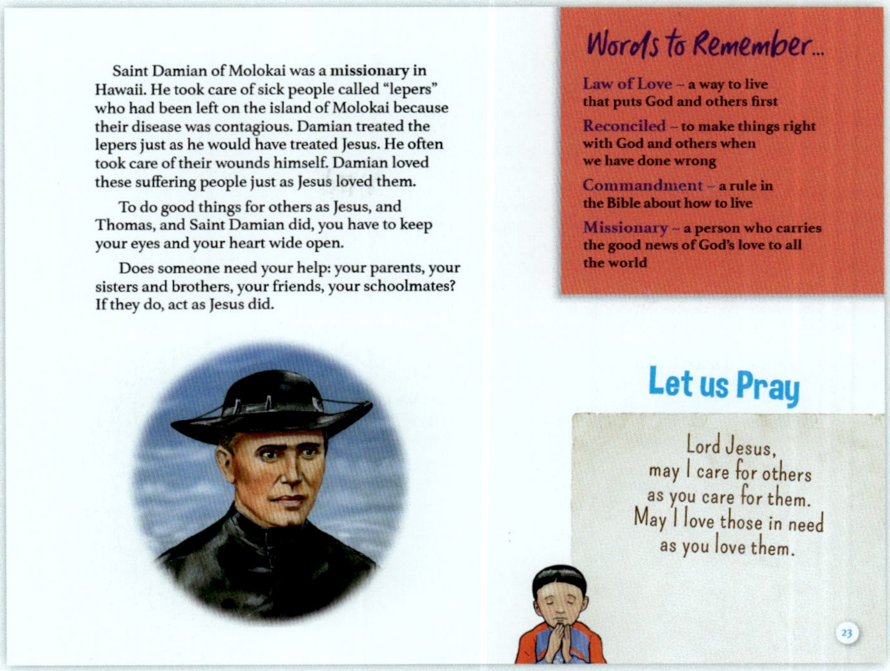

Saint Damian of Molokai was a **missionary** in Hawaii. He took care of sick people called "lepers" who had been left on the island of Molokai because their disease was contagious. Damian treated the lepers just as he would have treated Jesus. He often took care of their wounds himself. Damian loved these suffering people just as Jesus loved them.

To do good things for others as Jesus, and Thomas, and Saint Damian did, you have to keep your eyes and your heart wide open.

Does someone need your help: your parents, your sisters and brothers, your friends, your schoolmates? If they do, act as Jesus did.

Words to Remember...

Law of Love – a way to live that puts God and others first

Reconciled – to make things right with God and others when we have done wrong

Commandment – a rule in the Bible about how to live

Missionary – a person who carries the good news of God's love to all the world

Let us Pray

Lord Jesus,
may I care for others
as you care for them.
May I love those in need
as you love them.

23

FOCUS: **Love in action is the greatest love of all.**

GOAL **To introduce the children to someone who proved his love for others through heroic service**

- Read together the story of Saint Damian. He was an extraordinary example of someone who loves others. For more information about Damian, see below.
- Ask the children what they think it means to keep your "eyes and heart wide open."
- Pray the prayer aloud together, then have individual children read it slowly and dramatically. Read it a final time, adding gestures. For example:

Lord Jesus (*hands folded*),
may I care for others (*arms outstretched*),
as you care for them (*arms lifted high*).
May I love those in need (*arms folded across heart*),
as you love them (*hands folded*).

- Go over the "Words to Remember" one by one. Be sure the children can describe the terms in their own words. (Add them to your chart of "Words to Remember," if you have made one.)

Did You Know?

A Martyr for Love

Saint Damian de Veuster was born in Belgium in 1840. Also known as Saint Damian of Molokai, he was a Roman Catholic priest and a member of the Congregation of the Sacred Hearts of Jesus and Mary, a missionary religious order. Father Damian is known for caring for people with leprosy, a contagious bacterial disease (now called Hansen's Disease). These people had been dropped off by ship on a remote area of the island of Molokai, in Hawaii. Damian eventually contracted the disease himself, and died in 1889. He is known as a "martyr of charity." His feast day is May 10. Damian was canonized in 2009 by Pope Benedict XVI.

The Church Teaches...

From our childhood on, we grow more and more aware of God's Law of Love. We learn good habits and how to do good deeds.
– adapted for children from CCC #1784

Ways to Show Love

You are on a journey that is taking you closer to God. You are on your way to celebrating God's forgiveness in the sacrament of Reconciliation. Before you arrive at this sacrament, you have to practise how to love and forgive.

Read the stories below. What is the best way each child in the stories can show love?

Ned notices that his neighbours Alberto and Rafaela are sad. Alberto is crying.

"Why are you so sad?" Ned asks.

"Our mom just lost her job," Rafaela explained, "and Alberto's birthday is coming soon. He was supposed to have a party and now he can't."

What can Ned do to help? What can his family do?

24

THEME: Ways to Show Love
FOCUS: **Love is shown through good habits and good deeds!**

GOAL **To help the children learn to show love in action**

- Share "The Church Teaches" lesson by reading it to the children. Invite them to repeat it after you and then take turns proclaiming it in a loud and clear voice.
- Invite the children to read the first paragraph on page 24. Explain that the stories that follow will help them practise love and forgiveness—or at least start to think about doing it.
- Allow time for the children to write out what Ned can do. Invite them to share their answers.
- What do they think Emma should do?
- Should Eric and Marisol run right out the door to help their elderly neighbour? Why might that be dangerous? What *can* they do?
- What should Simon and his friends do?
- Encourage the children to be honest and sincere. What would they *really* do in such situations? What *should* they do if they follow Jesus? Ask: What would Jesus do?
- Go over the "Look and Listen" game on page 25. Encourage the children to play it with their family. You might want to send copies of it home with a note encouraging parents to participate.

Emma is playing in the driveway. Her toys are all spread out. Her neighbour Maria calls out, "Come and play with me!" Emma knows that if she leaves her toys where they are, her dad will have to get out of the car and move them when he gets home from work, but she wants to go and play with Maria right away. What will Emma do?

Simon and his friends are playing soccer in the park. Adam is watching from his wheelchair. He wants to play, but he can't run. What will Simon and his friends do?

Eric and Marisol look out the window one day. They see an old woman who lives nearby. She is always walking alone. Today she is carrying two bags of groceries. Eric and Marisol feel sorry for her. They tell their parents about her. How could they help their neighbour?

LOOK AND LISTEN

Here's a game you can play with your family to help you SEE and HEAR how to love one another better.

Everyone writes their name on a slip of paper and puts it in a bag. Then they each pick one name out of the bag, without showing it to the others. (If someone picks their own name, they put that slip of paper back and pick again.) For the next week, everyone does secret good deeds for the person whose name they picked. At the end of the week, have everyone try to guess who was doing these loving things for them.

25

Notes for Catechists

What Should We Examine?

Older Catholics were taught to use an examination of conscience before going to "confession." This practice is still a good idea, but sometimes we must also examine our lives through a larger lens: not just our individual sins, but our way of life as a whole. As catechists, we have been called by Jesus to be followers of the Way: a way of compassion and love, healing, and forgiveness. We must start taking Jesus seriously by loving our enemies, turning the other cheek, forgiving seventy times seven, blessing those who curse us, sharing what we have with the poor, and putting all our hope and trust in God. We are called to be the salt of the earth and light for the world.

(For a more theological explanation of conscience, see Catechism of the Catholic Church, *paragraphs 1776, 1777, 1779, and 1785.)*

Sharing Family Love

Benjamin is excited. His grandparents are coming for dinner! That means they will all sit at the table for a long time, sharing good food and family stories. "Hurray!" says his sister Michelle. "I love it when we have special meals."

We all love times of celebration. Every family has its own way of celebrating. Family traditions make special days even more special. A tradition is something passed down from grandparents to parents to children: certain actions, certain ways of celebrating, even certain stories that are told just the right way. Family meals are the best time to share your family traditions.

Ask your parents to plan a special meal, a time when you can share love and laughter.

Something to Think About

- Do you enjoy special celebrations and special meals? Why?
- What are your family's traditions?
- What can you SEE and HEAR around your family table?

THEME: Sharing Family Love

FOCUS: **Is sharing family love truly possible without sharing family meals?**

GOAL **To emphasize the importance of family meals and traditions**

- Read aloud the first paragraph about Benjamin. Then have the children read the rest of the text silently.
- Go through the "Something to Think About" questions one by one. Allow time for the children to share answers and experiences.
- Explain that "traditions" are things a family does for certain holidays or special occasions. For example, one family always shares birthday cake before opening presents. Another family opens presents first. Ask the children which family traditions they love the most.
- Have the children focus on the picture. Do they share meals as a family, too? Now ask each child to write a note to his or her parent(s), asking for a family meal or meals together on a regular basis. Each should say why they would like this to happen.
- Ask the children: If you were to have a special meal, who would you want to be there? Why? What would you talk about? What prayer would you say before the meal?

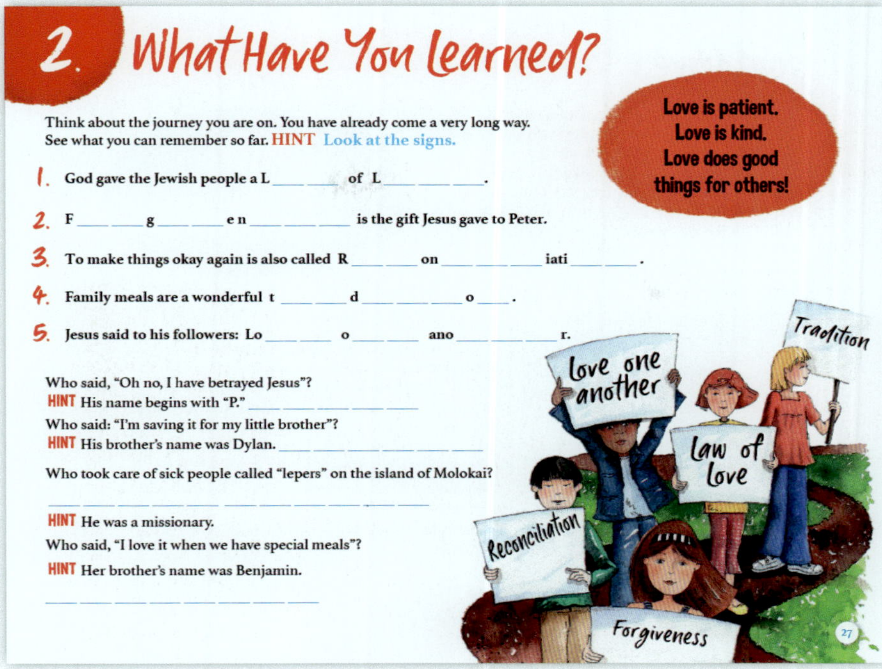

2. What Have You Learned?

Love is patient.
Love is kind.
Love does good things for others!

Think about the journey you are on. You have already come a very long way. See what you can remember so far. HINT Look at the signs.

1. God gave the Jewish people a L_____ of L_______.
2. F____ g_____ e n_______ is the gift Jesus gave to Peter.
3. To make things okay again is also called R______ on________ iati______.
4. Family meals are a wonderful t_____ d________ o___.
5. Jesus said to his followers: Lo_____ o_____ ano________ r.

Who said, "Oh no, I have betrayed Jesus"?
HINT His name begins with "P." ____________

Who said: "I'm saving it for my little brother"?
HINT His brother's name was Dylan. ____________

Who took care of sick people called "lepers" on the island of Molokai?
____
HINT He was a missionary.

Who said, "I love it when we have special meals"?
HINT Her brother's name was Benjamin.
____

THEME: *What Have You Learned?*
FOCUS: God's Gift of Love

GOAL To reinforce what the children have learned about love

- Invite the children to focus first on the words in the red oval. Have them repeat the words after you. Then invite individual children to proclaim them clearly and dramatically.
- Now focus on the illustration. Read the words on the signs. As you read each one, ask the children to define it in their own words. (Add them to your chart of "Words to Remember," if you have made one.)
- Ask the children to complete the five sentences, using the words on the signs as hints. Then go over each sentence to be sure they understand it.
- Now see if they remember the "Who Said" sentences. Encourage them to look back in their books to find the answers. Add some sentences of your own from past lessons if you wish.

Notes for Catechists

The Importance of Family Meals

We focus here on family meals because during meals, conversation happens and relationships between parents and children are strengthened. As part of this program, parents are invited to converse and pray with their child. For many, this will seem an impossible task unless they have a forum for family conversation and prayer, and a family meal is a beginning. As a catechist, you can encourage the children to ask their parents to share family meals more often.

3. God Gives You Joy

Isn't it great to know how much God loves you? Isn't it a blessing to know that God will always love you and forgive you, no matter what?

When you are loved and forgiven, you feel happy inside. This feeling is called **joy**. Jesus felt joy because he knew God his Father loved him. He talked to God all through his day – every day!

From the Bible

God, you are the joy of my heart!
~ Psalm 104:34

Estella was angry with her mother because she would not allow her to go to Sophia's house with her friends. "You're so unfair," cried Estella. "All the other kids get to go!"

That very day, one of Estella's friends fell and cut her arm at Sophia's house, and no adult was home to take her to the hospital. She was bleeding for a long time. That night Estella told her mother she was sorry for her angry words.

Her mother said, "I understand. It's hard to be left behind, but I want you to be safe. I forgive you for your anger."

Estella felt so relieved. She had a deep feeling of joy in her heart.

28

THEME: *God Gives You Joy*

FOCUS: **God invites all of us to experience joy to the fullest!**

GOAL **To introduce the children to the kind of joy Jesus experienced**

- Ask the children what joy is. What makes them feel joyful?
- Read the "From the Bible" words and have the children repeat them after you. Then invite each child to say the words again, adding a prayerful gesture. Offer suggestions: hands folded, arms crossed over chest, arms raised, head bowed, and kneeling.
- Read the first two paragraphs aloud, then ask: What gave Jesus joy?
- Now have the children take turns reading about Estella. Go over the "Something to Think About" questions on page 29. Invite the children to share their responses to the second question in particular. Ask if they noticed the picture on page 28. Have they ever felt loved and forgiven in this way?
- Read page 29 aloud, then ask the children to look at the illustration of Jesus. What is he doing? Why do they think he went off by himself to pray?
- Ask the children to close their eyes and think about this question: What does Jesus want to give you? Before they open their eyes, they are to think of an answer to share. After the sharing, invite them to read "From the Bible." Did anyone guess that Jesus wants to give joy?
- Read the first paragraph on page 29 again. Remind the children that Jesus' friends wanted to share his joy, so one day they said, "Lord, teach us how to pray." Jesus was happy to help them. (In the next section, the children will study the Our Father, the prayer that Jesus taught his friends.)

When he taught the people, Jesus always spoke about God. He told them that his Father was always with him, and that's why he was so full of joy.

Many times, Jesus would go off by himself to find a quiet place to pray. When his friends looked for him, they often found him alone on a hillside talking to God.

Jesus' friends wanted to share his joy, so one day they said, "Lord, teach us how to pray." Jesus was happy to help them.

Something to Think About

- Why do you think Jesus wanted to be alone to pray?
- Have you ever felt the joy of being loved and forgiven?

From the Bible

Jesus said to his friends, "I want my joy to be in you."
~ adapted from John 15:11

29

Did You Know?

The Virtue of Joy

Psalm 81 begins this way: "Sing aloud to God who is our strength; shout for joy to our God." Though we often use the word "happiness" in place of joy, they are not the same. Joy is more profound and lasting. It is a spiritual awareness that God is with us that remains even in difficult times. St. Paul calls joy a fruit of the Holy Spirit, along with love, peace, patience, kindness, generosity, faithfulness, gentleness, and self-control (Galatians 5:22-23). Pray often for the gift of joy, especially in your role as a catechist.

The Lord's Prayer

Here are the prayer words that Jesus gave his friends.
This prayer is also called the Our Father.

Our Father...	You are the Father of Jesus, but we, too, are your children. You know our names and love us very much. We can talk to you any time, the way we would talk to the most loving father or mother.
Who art in heaven...	Heaven is your home, the place of light where you live. But you also live in our hearts and you are always with us.
Hallowed be thy name...	When we say your name, God, we are speaking of the most wonderful being who exists. So we pray that your name will always be loved and respected by everyone.
Thy kingdom come...	Where you are in heaven, there is always joy. We ask that the same joy be in us. May we have this joy now, here on earth, and share it with others.
Thy will be done on earth as it is in heaven...	You know what is best for us. You always show us the right way. May we always follow your Law of Love.

30

THEME: *The Lord's Prayer*

FOCUS: **This is the prayer Jesus gave his followers when they asked him how to pray.**

GOAL **To teach the children to memorize and pray the Our Father**

- Go over each phrase of this prayer with the children. Explain it to them as it is explained on pages 30 and 31.
- Say each phrase aloud, one at a time, then have the children repeat it after you. Spend time helping them memorize each phrase (and do this again in subsequent sessions). You might want to give the children copies of the Our Father with a note to parents to help them memorize it.
- Share with the children that Christians all over the world pray the Our Father every day. Together, read "The Church Teaches" on page 31. Explain that because Jesus' followers called him "Lord," the Our Father is known as the Lord's Prayer.
- Invite the children to look at the illustrations on pages 30 and 31, beginning with the ones on the left. Ask them to imitate, one by one, the gestures the children in the illustrations are making. Which of these are they most comfortable with? Ask each child to choose one and use this gesture as you pray the Our Father together. Choose one for yourself as well.
- Ask one of the children to read "The Church Teaches" on page 31, and then have all the children read it together. If you have not already explained to them that the *Catechism of the Catholic Church* explains what we believe as Catholics, point that out now. If you have a copy of the Catechism, show it to them. Explain that the statement in their book comes from this Catechism.

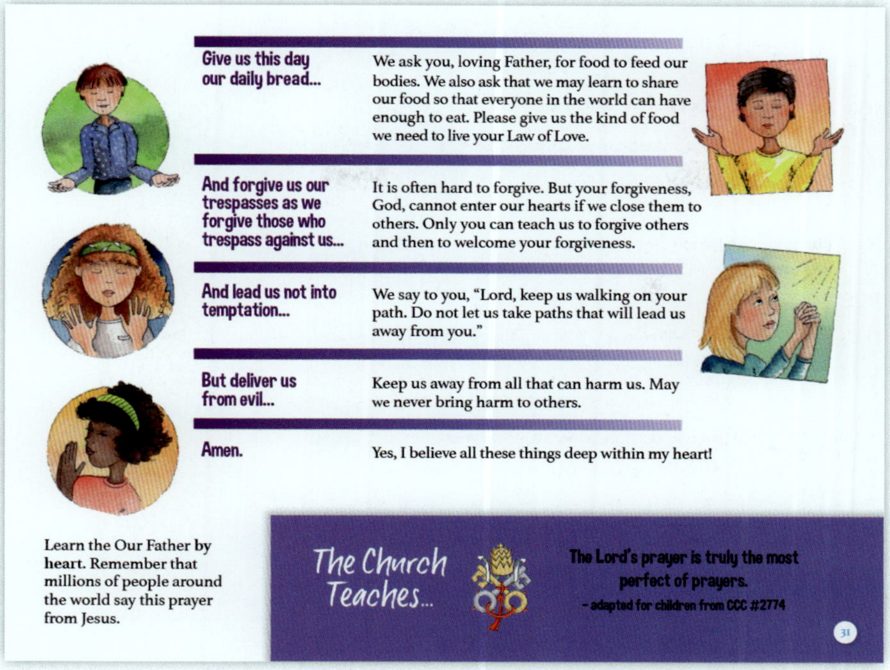

Give us this day our daily bread...	We ask you, loving Father, for food to feed our bodies. We also ask that we may learn to share our food so that everyone in the world can have enough to eat. Please give us the kind of food we need to live your Law of Love.
And forgive us our trespasses as we forgive those who trespass against us...	It is often hard to forgive. But your forgiveness, God, cannot enter our hearts if we close them to others. Only you can teach us to forgive others and then to welcome your forgiveness.
And lead us not into temptation...	We say to you, "Lord, keep us walking on your path. Do not let us take paths that will lead us away from you."
But deliver us from evil...	Keep us away from all that can harm us. May we never bring harm to others.
Amen.	Yes, I believe all these things deep within my heart!

Learn the Our Father by heart. Remember that millions of people around the world say this prayer from Jesus.

The Church Teaches...

The Lord's prayer is truly the most perfect of prayers.
– adapted for children from CCC #2774

31

Did You Know?

A Prayer that Unites

The Lord's Prayer or Our Father is probably the best-known Christian prayer. Although Christians do not always agree, and they worship in different ways, the fact that Christians around the globe pray the Our Father together gives a sense of solidarity. Two versions of this prayer are found in the Gospels: in Matthew 6:9-13 and in Luke 11:2-4.

Notes for Catechists

More About Prayer

- Designate one place in your teaching area as the prayer space. This can be a desk, a small stand, or a portable table. Gather in this space for your class prayer.
- Use prayers from the Mass and other liturgical rites. (The liturgy is under-taught, so use prayers and rituals from it often to reinforce their meaning.)
- Use background music from time to time to create an atmosphere of calm and quiet.

Many Ways to Pray

Jesus' joy came from being very close to God his Father. Talking to God helped keep his joy alive. Jesus wants to share his joy with us, and so he gives us a helper called the Holy Spirit to remind us to pray often. Here are some of the ways people pray with the help of the Holy Spirit.

From the Bible

Jesus told his friends, "When two or three of you gather in my name, I am with you."
~ adapted from Matthew 18:20

Connor must hurry in the morning, but he always takes a few moments to say good morning to God.

At Rosa and Mario's home, the family prays together before supper.

32

THEME: *Many Ways to Pray*

FOCUS: Prayer is the glue that cements our day.

GOAL To help the children experience a variety of ways to talk to God

- Pray the Our Father together. If the children have not yet memorized it, say each phrase and have them repeat it after you.
- Read the first paragraph on page 32. If you have not yet mentioned or discussed the Holy Spirit (such as when the children learned the Sign of the Cross and the Glory to God), simply explain to the children that this is one of the names of God. When Jesus left this world to return to heaven, he sent his Spirit to be with us always. This is the Holy Spirit. The Holy Spirit helps us to remember that God is with us. Jesus told his followers, "The Holy Spirit will teach you everything and remind you of all that I have said to you." (John 14:26)
- Read the sentence about Connor and then talk about the picture. Do the children say "Good morning" to God? In what ways?
- Read about Rosa and Mario. Do the children pray at meals? Would they like to? What could they say?
- Point out the colourful cross on this page. Explain that religious symbols such as the cross are reminders that Jesus is always with us and we can pray to him. Ask: Are there reminders of Jesus and God in your home? Where are they? (Remind the children that their prayer corners are such places—or can be.)
- Read the paragraph about Simon on page 33, which illustrates that we can pray no matter what: when we are busy, when we are happy, when we are angry, when we are sad. Ask the children when they pray each day. What is the best time for them to pray?
- Now read the final paragraph and focus on the illustration. When we pray at Mass, God is there with us in Jesus. He brings us together to pray, to sing, and to share the Lord's Supper.

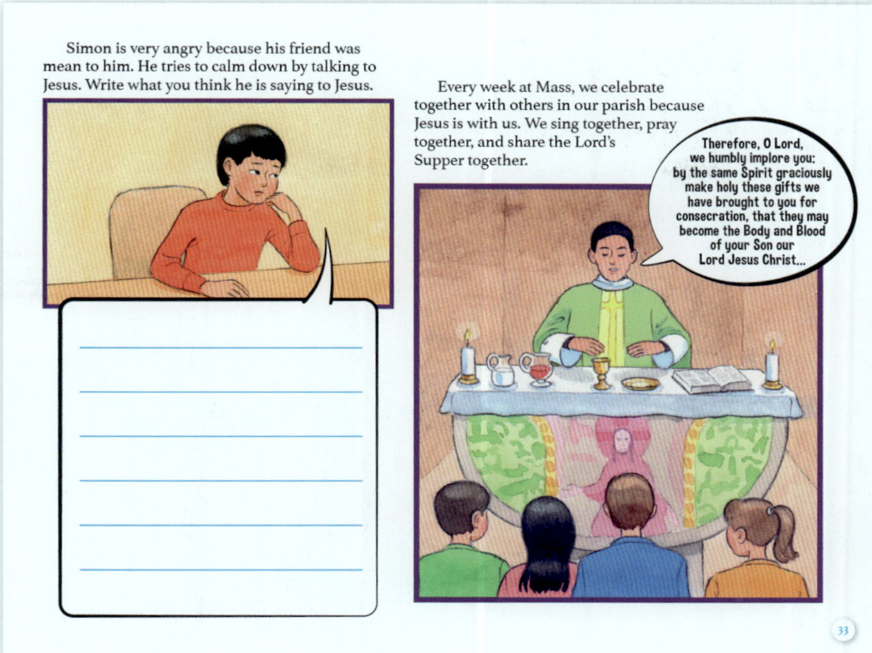

- Ask the children to name some of the ways they can pray. Then turn to the words "From the Bible" on page 32. Read them first and have the children repeat the words after you. Then invite them to proclaim these words loudly and clearly.
- Before the children leave, bless each of them with the Sign of the Cross as you say, "Remember that God, Father, Son, and Holy Spirit, is always with you." Each can answer, "Amen."

Notes for Catechists

Your Own Prayer

At a meeting in 2009, Catholic bishops recommended that Catholic adults use a form of prayer called Lectio Divina, Latin for "divine reading," "spiritual reading," or "holy reading." This traditional Christian practice of prayer and scriptural reading draws us closer to God through Scripture. This is a way of praying with Scripture that invites us to study, ponder, listen, and commune with God.

Study: Read a scripture passage slowly and attentively several times.

Ponder: Focus on something in the passage that caught your attention and quietly let it sink in.

Listen: Take time to open your heart and converse with God.

Commune: Having a simple, loving focus on God, resting in God's presence.

Learning About Quiet Prayer

There are many ways to pray. All of them bring great peace and joy. All of them bring us closer to God. Jesus often prayed in a quiet place.

If you would like to try **quiet prayer**, here's what you can do:

- Sit down facing your prayer corner or other quiet place.
- Close your eyes.
- Breathe slowly and deeply a few times until you feel quiet inside.
- Remember that Jesus is with you.
- In a very soft voice, or in your heart, slowly say a short prayer. Say it over and over, as often as you like. Some people say the name "Jesus" until the peace of God fills their hearts.
- Sit still for as long as you like and share with God whatever is in your heart.

From the Bible

Jesus, full of the Holy Spirit, was led into the wilderness to fast and pray.
~ adapted from Luke 4:1

34

THEME: *Learning About Quiet Prayer*

FOCUS: **Children, too, can commune with God.**

GOAL **To introduce the children to silent prayer as a way of talking with God**

- Pray the Our Father together. If the children have not yet memorized it, have them repeat it after you.
- Read the first paragraph together, then focus on the "From the Bible" words. This is the way Jesus sometimes chose to pray, off by himself. Here, "wilderness" describes a private place where he could be alone with God.
- Invite the children to pray as Jesus might have prayed when he was alone. Have them look at the illustration to see one way to do this. Or they can simply sit in a chair (or on their bed, when at home). Explain that they need to sit in silence so they do not disturb others. Begin when everyone is settled and quiet.
- Walk them through the six steps and allow sufficient time for each. Once you reach the final step, wrap up the prayer time when the children get restless.
- Invite comments about this way of prayer. Did they like it? Can they try it at home in their prayer corner or in their room?
- If possible, send a note to parents asking them to help their children practise this prayer (as on page 34 of the child's book).

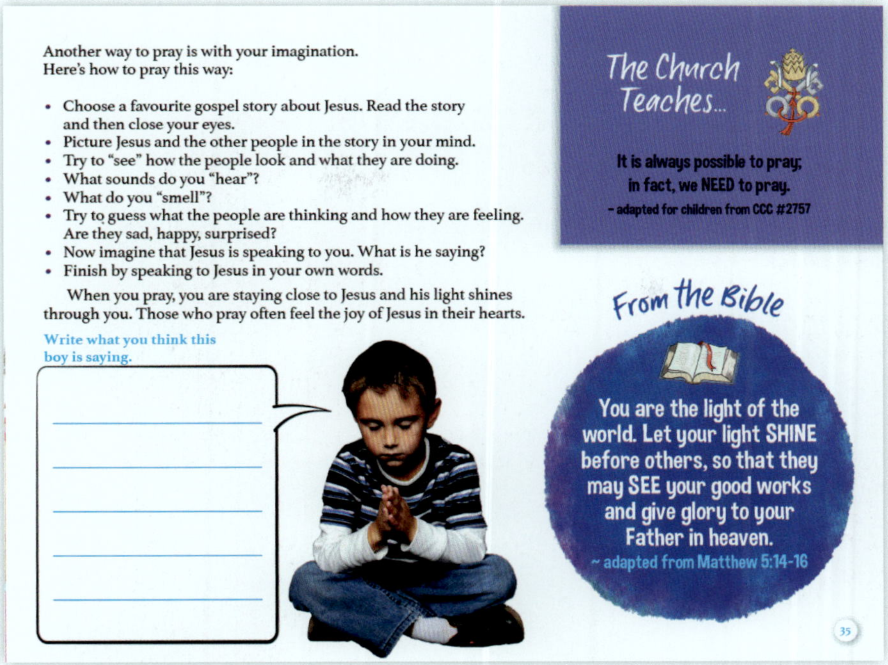

Another way to pray is with your imagination.
Here's how to pray this way:

- Choose a favourite gospel story about Jesus. Read the story and then close your eyes.
- Picture Jesus and the other people in the story in your mind.
- Try to "see" how the people look and what they are doing.
- What sounds do you "hear"?
- What do you "smell"?
- Try to guess what the people are thinking and how they are feeling. Are they sad, happy, surprised?
- Now imagine that Jesus is speaking to you. What is he saying?
- Finish by speaking to Jesus in your own words.

When you pray, you are staying close to Jesus and his light shines through you. Those who pray often feel the joy of Jesus in their hearts.

Write what you think this boy is saying.

The Church Teaches...

It is always possible to pray; in fact, we NEED to pray.
– adapted for children from CCC #2757

From the Bible

You are the light of the world. Let your light SHINE before others, so that they may SEE your good works and give glory to your Father in heaven.
~ adapted from Matthew 5:14-16

35

FOCUS: **Children with active imaginations love this form of prayer.**

GOAL **To help the children experience prayer in a more light-hearted way**

- Share "The Church Teaches" by reading the words loudly and clearly. Have the children repeat them after you. Then you say the first part and they loudly say, "We need to pray!" Do this several times.
- Review some of the ways the children have already experienced prayer: the Sign of the Cross, the Glory to God, the Our Father, talking to God throughout the day, gathering to pray at Mass, and quiet prayer. Invite them to comment on these ways to pray. Which do they like best? Which have they tried at home? Which would they like to try more often?
- Now introduce a new way to pray: the prayer of imagination. Ask the children to explain what "imagination" is.
- Choose a favourite gospel story, such as Matthew 19:13-15, the blessing of the children. Explain before you begin reading that "laying his hands on them" means blessing the children, as you sometimes do in class.
- Read the passage aloud slowly and clearly, then walk through the steps with them, beginning with "Picture Jesus..." (page 35 of the child's book). Take your time; this exercise cannot be rushed.
- Invite comments about this way of prayer. Did they like it? Will they try it at home in their prayer corner?
- Read the final two sentences on this page, then call attention to the "From the Bible" words. Emphasize the words "shine" and "see." Then have the children say this passage after you.

Mary's Prayer

Mary is Jesus' mother. She is our mother, too. She asks God to watch over each of us. Mary talked to God often when she was a young woman. One day, the angel Gabriel came to visit her. (An angel is one who brings a message from God.) Gabriel told Mary that God wanted her to be the mother of Jesus. Mary said, "Yes, I will do whatever God asks of me."

The Church has a special prayer to Mary called the **Hail Mary.** Millions of Catholics all over the world pray this prayer every day! You can pray it as often as you like. Invite your family to pray it with you.

Let us Pray

Learn this prayer by heart.

Hail Mary, full of grace,
the Lord is with you.

Blessed are you among women
and blessed is the fruit of
your womb, Jesus.

Holy Mary, Mother of God,
pray for us sinners,
now and at the hour
of our death.
Amen.

THEME: *Mary's Prayer*

FOCUS: **The Hail Mary is both a prayer of praise and a prayer of petition.**

GOAL **To teach the children about Mary and the Hail Mary**

- Ask the children what they know about Mary. Who was she? Why do we love and honour her? What does she teach us?
- Read the first paragraph aloud. Share that Mary probably prayed often. She had her eyes and heart open to God. When God spoke to her through the angel, she listened. She said "yes" to God.
- Look at the illustration together. Invite the children to comment on it. What do they see? How does Mary look? How does the angel look?
- Read the second paragraph aloud. The Hail Mary is a revered traditional prayer that children should learn by heart.
- Now pray each line of the Hail Mary, with the children repeating it after you. (Tell them that the first part of this prayer is drawn from the Gospel of Luke [Luke 1:26-35]). Then have them read the words together several times. If possible, send a note to parents encouraging them to help their child learn this prayer by praying it together often.

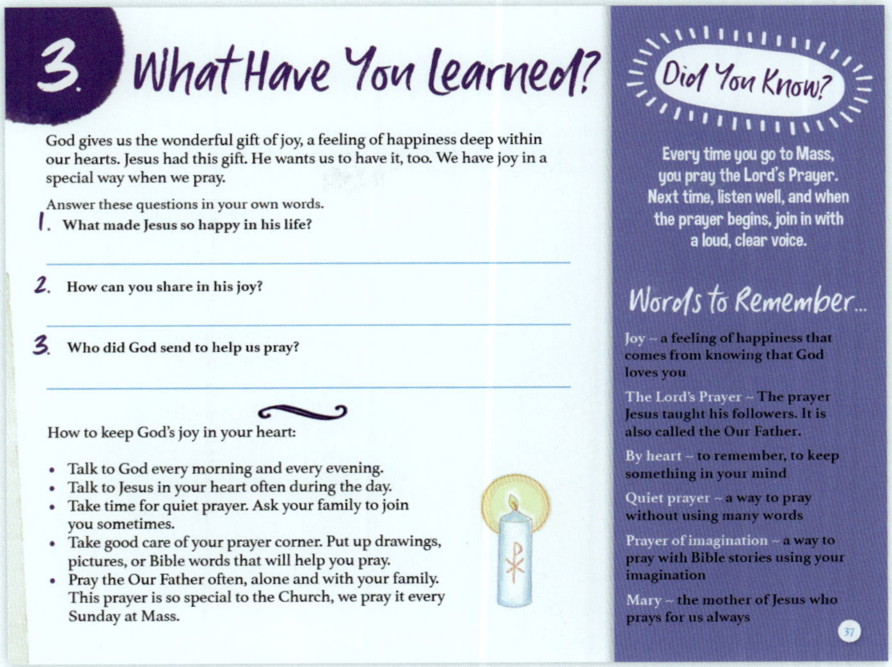

3. What Have You Learned?

God gives us the wonderful gift of joy, a feeling of happiness deep within our hearts. Jesus had this gift. He wants us to have it, too. We have joy in a special way when we pray.

Answer these questions in your own words.

1. What made Jesus so happy in his life?
2. How can you share in his joy?
3. Who did God send to help us pray?

How to keep God's joy in your heart:

- Talk to God every morning and every evening.
- Talk to Jesus in your heart often during the day.
- Take time for quiet prayer. Ask your family to join you sometimes.
- Take good care of your prayer corner. Put up drawings, pictures, or Bible words that will help you pray.
- Pray the Our Father often, alone and with your family. This prayer is so special to the Church, we pray it every Sunday at Mass.

Did You Know?

Every time you go to Mass, you pray the Lord's Prayer. Next time, listen well, and when the prayer begins, join in with a loud, clear voice.

Words to Remember...

Joy – a feeling of happiness that comes from knowing that God loves you

The Lord's Prayer – The prayer Jesus taught his followers. It is also called the Our Father.

By heart – to remember, to keep something in your mind

Quiet prayer – a way to pray without using many words

Prayer of imagination – a way to pray with Bible stories using your imagination

Mary – the mother of Jesus who prays for us always

37

THEME: What Have You Learned?

FOCUS: God's Gift of Joy

GOAL To offer the children the opportunity to revisit what they have learned about joy

- Read the first paragraph aloud, then go over the three questions with the children. If they need to look back for answers, encourage them to do so.
- Talk about ways to keep God's joy in their hearts. As you or a child read each suggestion, ask the children to comment: Do they already do these things? In what ways? At what times and in what places?
- Now review the "Words to Remember." (Add them to your chart of "Words to Remember," if you have made one.) Be sure the children can define each term in their own words, or at least have an idea of its meaning.
- Ask a child to read "Did You Know?" Then pray the Our Father together. Have the children raise their cupped hands as they pray it.
- Close by making the Sign of the Cross together. Be sure the children are using the right motions for this gesture.

Notes for Catechists

More About Prayer

When you use formal prayers with children, try to keep prayer lively and not routine. Here are a few things to try:

- Invite the children to close their eyes and recall the presence of God before you say a formal prayer. (Never use formal prayers to silence children.)
- Share celebrations of the Word by carrying the Bible in procession to your prayer space and proclaiming the Scripture passage used in your lesson. Invite the children to take turns proclaiming the Word. Encourage them to speak slowly and clearly.

4. God Gives You Peace

Everyone wants to be happy and get along with others. We all like to feel peaceful and happy. That's what God wants for us, too. This is God's great dream, the dream that Jesus came to tell us about: "Stay close to God and God's plan for you, and you will have peace and joy in your life."

From the Bible

Have mercy on me, O God, because I am weak and I have sinned.
~ adapted from Psalm 106:6

38

THEME: God Gives You Peace

FOCUS: **When we are truly forgiven, peace settles in our hearts.**

GOAL **To introduce the concept of sin as something that diminishes peace and well-being**

- Ask the children to focus on the illustration. How does everyone look: happy, sad, angry, peaceful? Why do they think the people look this way?
- Now read the text. Repeat the words "Stay close to God…", then have the children repeat them after you line by line.
- Share the "From the Bible" words. Explain that sin or doing wrong keeps us from feeling God's peace. These words are asking God to make things right. Tell the children that sin also hurts our relationships with family, friends, classmates, and others.
- Call attention to the dove on page 39.. It is a sign of the Holy Spirit, a sign of peace and balance, feelings we have when we live in harmony with God and others. Invite the children to draw a dove of their own, decorate it, and print within it the word "peace." They can place this drawing in their prayer corner at home as a reminder that God gives them peace.
- Now ask the children to focus on the picture on page 39. Is there a difference in how the people look? Why? What happened? Ask them to think about this for a moment.
- Invite the children to read the text aloud, taking turns sentence by sentence. Emphasize this line: "When we sin, we cause pain and suffering instead of peace and happiness." Have the children focus on the illustration again and discuss it in light of what they have just read.
- Share "The Church Teaches" on page 39 by saying it loudly and clearly. Then have the children repeat it after you. Remind them that God's plan is one of love, joy, peace, and forgiveness.

The Church Teaches...

When we sin, we choose our own plan over God's plan for us.
- adapted for children from CCC #398

But sometimes things happen and we turn away from God's love. Whether we are children or grown-ups, we may do or say things to others that hurt them.

- We take something that is not ours.
- We cheat or we lie.
- We disobey our parents or teachers.
- We hurt other people's feelings.

To say this in another way, we choose **sin**.

When we sin, we cause pain and suffering instead of peace and happiness.

Here are some stories about what happens when we turn away from God.

39

A Prayer for You

Loving and forgiving God,
as I move with these children
towards the experience of peace
and reconciliation,
open my mind and heart to your light.
Help me to find the words to welcome them
into your forgiving embrace.
Help me to convey an attitude
of joy in your forgiveness
and a desire for your peace in their hearts.
Guide me, loving God, as I guide these children
towards your Law of Love.
Amen.

When You Disobey

Amelia and her mom have just moved to a new house. Amelia's grandparents are coming to see it. There is a lot of work to do before they arrive. Amelia's mom has to hang up some curtains and then prepare a special supper.

But once Amelia gets outside...

40

THEME: When You Disobey

FOCUS: **It is easy to take the wrong road when we make decisions.**

GOAL **To provide concrete examples of selfish behaviour (*this is the goal for pages 40 to 43*)**

- Read the text together. Be sure the children understand the context.
- Focus on the illustrations and the commentary on page 40. Have the children take turns reading the text aloud. Ask what they think Amelia might do. What would *they* do?
- Now go to the illustrations and speech bubbles on page 41. What *did* Amelia do?
- Go over the "Something to Think About" questions on page 41. Focus on the second one. Explain that *not* doing what we are asked, *not* helping when there is a need, and *not* taking care of our rooms, for example, are ways we hurt others. God's Law of Love asks us to think of others first, and do more for them, rather than less.

Something to Think About

- Why did Amelia disobey her mother?
- Did her actions hurt anyone?
- Do you think Amelia followed God's Law of Love?

41

Notes for Catechists

Kids Will Be Kids

Many children would do exactly as Amelia did and follow the impulse to play rather than to return home and get ready for guests. Here we are suggesting that Amelia was not sinful so much as selfish. Children must be guided in their small daily choices towards God's Law of Love so that when major choices loom, they can choose the better part: unselfish love. Here are some things for you to think about:

- Omission is, in Catholic teaching, the failure to do something one can and ought to do. If this happens advertently and freely, a sin is committed. The degree of guilt incurred by an omission depends on how serious and deliberate it was.
- A person may be guilty of a sin of omission by failing to do something because of a choice he or she makes. For example, a person who knows that drinking to the point of drunkenness will leave him or her unable to care for his or her children, and yet drinks anyway, has sinned.
- Paul the Apostle refers to this type of sin directly when he says, "I do not do the good I want ..." (Romans 7:19).

When You Hurt Others

Caleb got a remote-control car for his birthday. All the kids really liked it.

Later, James noticed that Caleb had left his car in the cloakroom.

Something to Think About

- Why would James do something like this to his friend?
- How do you think James felt about it?
- Do you think James was following God's dream for him?

No one was around, so James took the car.

At the end of the day, Caleb couldn't find his car. He asked his friends about it.

42

THEME: When You Hurt Others

- Share each scenario by asking the children to take turns reading them aloud.
- Go over the "Something to Think About" questions for the scenarios. Give the children time to think about their answers and to share personal experiences. Focus on question three and ask, "Why or why not?"
- Again, share each scenario by asking the children to take turns reading them aloud.
- Now read aloud the paragraph at the top right of page 43. Then have the children read it after you, phrase by phrase.

Notes for Catechists

More About Prayer

There are many beautiful prayers in the Catholic tradition, such as the Hail Mary, Our Father, Glory to God, Act of Contrition, and the prayers of the Mass. When you pray with children:

- Divide prayers into parts and have the children read them in chorus.
- "Chant" formal prayers instead of simply reciting them. (Chanting is done by choosing one note or tone and saying/singing the prayer that way.)

A Prayer for You

Jesus, you are the light of the world
from which I draw my light.
Without you, I have no light.
You are the Word of God
from which I draw my teaching.
Without you, I have no words.
You are the way, the truth, and the life
from which I draw my ministry.
Without you, I have nothing to teach.
Share your gifts with me, please,
that I might draw the children I teach
to your light, your Word, your Way.
Amen.

When Stephanie tries to read, all the letters look mixed up.

Yesterday, the teacher asked her to read out loud in class. She made mistakes right away.

Behind her, Lydia and Christine started making fun of her. Stephanie heard them. She stopped reading and started to cry.

In God's Law of Love, there is no place for sin. When you do wrong, you hurt yourself and others. God loves you and wants you to be happy. God wants you to turn away from sin.

Something to Think About

- Is it okay to make fun of someone? Why or why not?
- How do you feel when someone makes fun of you?
- Do you think Lydia and Christine were following God's dream for them?

43

Notes for Catechists

What Is Sin?

Here is how the *Catechism of the Catholic Church* defines sin:

> Sin is an offense against reason, truth and right conscience; it is failure in genuine love for God and neighbour caused by a perverse attachment to certain goods. It wounds the nature of [a person] and injures human solidarity. It has been defined as "an utterance, a deed or a desire contrary to the eternal law." (#1849)

Here are some definitions of sin:

1. A transgression of a religious or moral law, especially when deliberate.
2. Deliberate disobedience to the known will of God.
3. A condition of estrangement from God resulting from such disobedience.
4. Something regarded as being shameful, deplorable, or utterly wrong.
5. How would you define sin? In the child's book, we define it as an action we do on purpose that turns us away from God and hurts others. Children don't need the theological definitions above; it is enough for them to know that sin damages our relationships with God and others.

God Always Guides You

Did you know? God has placed a small voice inside you that helps you know what is right or wrong. This voice is called your **conscience.** In the Bible, God gives rules that help your conscience make good choices. These are called the **Ten Commandments.** They are mostly for grown-ups, but you can learn them, too. In the gospels, Jesus gives us rules that will keep us on the path to God and help our **conscience** to learn God's Law of Love. We call these rules **gospel teachings.**

44

The Ten Commandments

1. **Love God with all your heart.**
2. **Do not curse or swear.**
3. **Remember that Sunday is a holy day.**
4. **Love and respect your parents.**
5. **Respect all life.**
6. **Be a good and faithful husband or wife.**
7. **Do not steal from others.**
8. **Do not tell lies.**
9. **Do not be jealous of what others have.**
10. **Respect your neighbours and all that is theirs.**

– adapted from Exodus 20:1-21

THEME: God Always Guides You

FOCUS: **God does not leave us alone to make our decisions, but rather gives us guidelines to follow.**

GOAL **To introduce the children to some of the "rules" God gives us to help us make right choices (*this is also the goal for page 45*)**

- Introduce the concept of conscience by saying, "Now I want to tell you something important. When you go home today, try to be as nasty as possible." Quickly ask, "What do you think about what I've just said? How did you react to it? Did you feel that what I said was wrong? Why? What told you it was wrong?" (Give them time to answer each question before you move to the next one.)
- Now read the text. Have the children take turns reading, sentence by sentence.
- Read the Ten Commandments and have the children repeat them after you. Then assign one commandment to each child. Have them proclaim it with a loud, clear voice. (*Note that the wording here is adapted for children. If you want to share the originals, see Exodus 20:1-21.*)
- Direct the children to the rules from Jesus on page 45. Point out that these "rules" are based on doing more for others, reaching out to others, giving unselfish love. They can be summed up by the last line: "Love one another as I have loved you." Again, read them aloud, then assign one to each child for proclaiming.

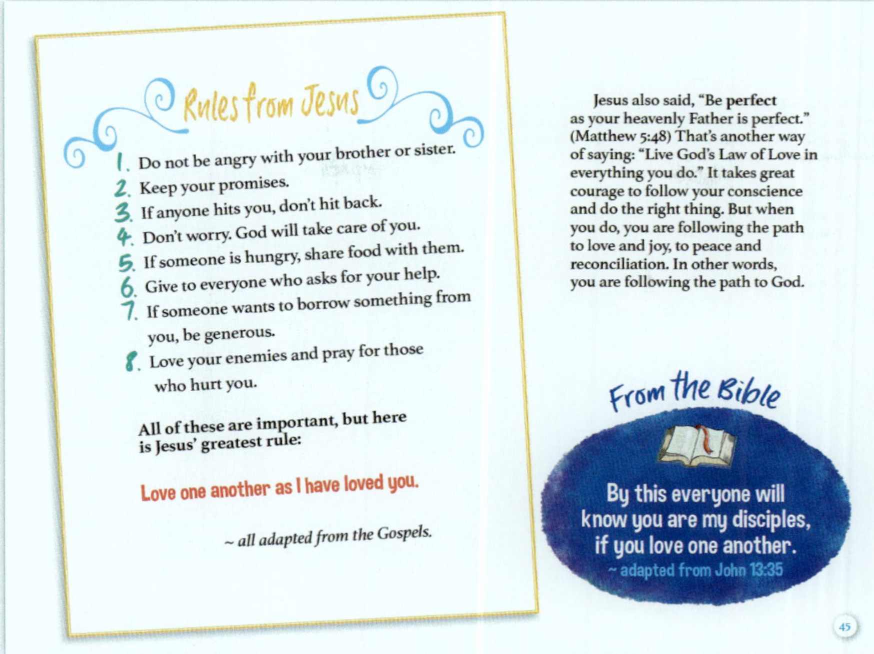

Rules from Jesus

1. Do not be angry with your brother or sister.
2. Keep your promises.
3. If anyone hits you, don't hit back.
4. Don't worry. God will take care of you.
5. If someone is hungry, share food with them.
6. Give to everyone who asks for your help.
7. If someone wants to borrow something from you, be generous.
8. Love your enemies and pray for those who hurt you.

All of these are important, but here is Jesus' greatest rule:

Love one another as I have loved you.

~ all adapted from the Gospels.

Jesus also said, "Be **perfect** as your heavenly Father is perfect." (Matthew 5:48) That's another way of saying: "Live God's Law of Love in everything you do." It takes great courage to follow your conscience and do the right thing. But when you do, you are following the path to love and joy, to peace and reconciliation. In other words, you are following the path to God.

From the Bible

By this everyone will know you are my disciples, if you love one another.
~ adapted from John 13:35

45

- Share the "From the Bible" words, then ask the children what they think Jesus meant by these words. He was talking to his followers. A word for followers of Jesus is "disciples." Explain that "disciples" are people who follow Jesus and thus love others.
- Read the text on the top right. Be sure the children listened well by asking, "What is courage? What is your conscience? What is the path to God?"

God Always Forgives You

Jesus teaches that when we have sinned, we should always return to God our Father because God never stops loving us. Many times during his life, Jesus forgave people who had sinned. He asked them to return to God's Law of Love.

One day some people brought a woman to Jesus. She had been caught doing something very wrong. They wanted Jesus to punish her. Instead, he forgave the woman and told her to sin no more.

THEME: *God Always Forgives You*

FOCUS: **As God's Son and messenger, Jesus taught us to forgive and forgive again.**

GOAL **To teach the children that Jesus forgave people and asked them to "return to God's Law of Love"**

- Read the text at the top of the page. Then look at the illustrations. Have the children comment on what is happening in each one. Then read the next paragraph. Explain that "sin no more" means to return to God's Law of Love.
- Have the children take turns reading aloud the first paragraph on page 47. Here you are introducing a particular way that God forgives us: the sacrament of Reconciliation.
- Invite the children to close their eyes and think of a time when they did something wrong on purpose, something that hurt another person. What happened afterwards? Did someone forgive them?

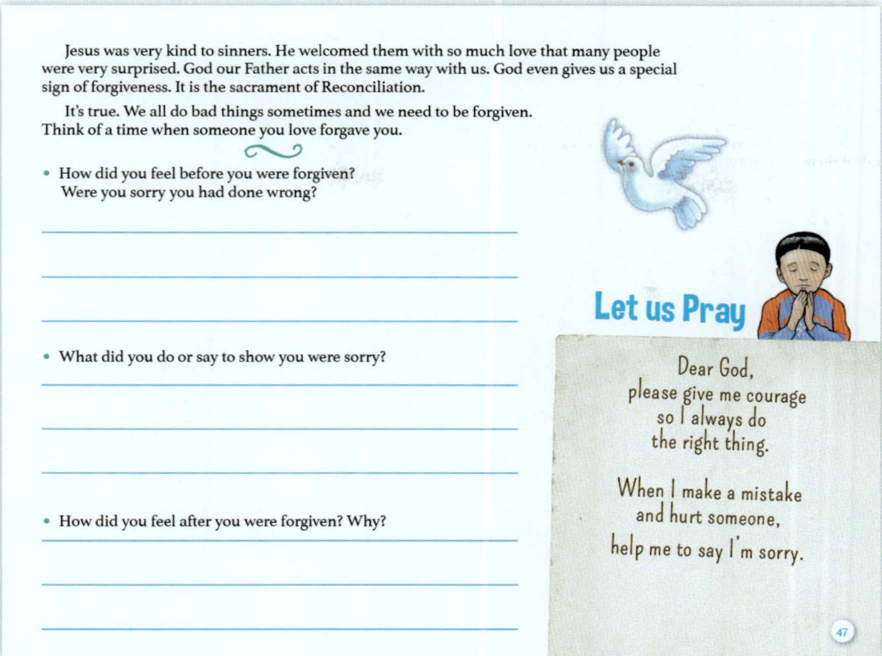

Jesus was very kind to sinners. He welcomed them with so much love that many people were very surprised. God our Father acts in the same way with us. God even gives us a special sign of forgiveness. It is the sacrament of Reconciliation.

It's true. We all do bad things sometimes and we need to be forgiven. Think of a time when someone you love forgave you.

- How did you feel before you were forgiven? Were you sorry you had done wrong?

- What did you do or say to show you were sorry?

- How did you feel after you were forgiven? Why?

Let us Pray

Dear God,
please give me courage
so I always do
the right thing.

When I make a mistake
and hurt someone,
help me to say I'm sorry.

47

- Have them write their responses to the three questions on the lines provided. Allow time for writing and discussion.
- Ask the children to look at the dove on this page. As already noted, a dove is a symbol of the Holy Spirit and of peace. Ask: Did you feel peace after you were forgiven? Give them sheets of paper so they can draw how forgiveness makes them feel. Ask them to include this prayer on their drawings: "Holy Spirit, please give me your peace."
- Now focus on the "Let us Pray" words. Pray them aloud and then have the children repeat them after you.

God Invites You to Change

God forgives us with love when we are truly sorry for our sins. But God also wants us to ask those we have hurt to forgive us. God wants us to change the way we treat others.

Read the stories on pages 40, 41, 42, and 43 one more time. How could the children make up for what they did?

What do you think?

- How could Amelia make up for disobeying her mother?

- How could James make up for stealing from Caleb and lying to him?

- How could Lydia and Christine make up for hurting Stephanie?

48

THEME: God Invites You to Change

FOCUS: It's never enough to say "sorry"; we must also make amends.

GOAL To help the children focus on ways to make amends when they have hurt others

- Read the first paragraph and tell the children that they will be reviewing some of the stories about other children and thinking of ways those children can make up for the wrong they did.
- Give them time to read Amelia's story (pages 40–41) and to answer the question on the lines provided.
- Have them read James's story (page 42) and answer the question.
- Invite them to do the same with Stephanie's story (page 43).
- Allow time for questions or concerns about ways to make up for things we have done wrong on purpose.

4. What Have You Learned?

You are now getting closer to the day when you will celebrate the sacrament of Reconciliation for the first time. Can you remember some of the things you have learned?

1. When you do something wrong on purpose, this is called a ___ ___ ___.
2. God does not want you to sin, because when you do, you ___ ___ ___ ___ others and yourself, too.
3. God is always ready to f___r g___ ___ ___ you because God never stops l___v___ ___ ___ you.
4. We can tell right from wrong because God has given us a c___ ___scie___ ___ ___.
5. One of the ways we form our conscience is by remembering the ___ ___ ___C___mm___ ___ ___ments.
6. Another way is by remembering Jesus' t___ ___ ___ ___ings in the gospels.

(Check your answers at the bottom of the page.)

ANSWERS: 1. sin 2. hurt 3. forgive, loving 4. conscience 5. Ten Commandments 6. teachings

Words to Remember...

Sin – an action we do on purpose that turns us away from God and hurts others

Ten Commandments – laws that God gave to the Jewish people

Gospel teachings – guidelines or rules that Jesus gave us to stay close to God

Conscience – a small inner voice that God placed in our hearts to help us know right from wrong

Being "perfect" – living God's Law of Love

49

THEME: What Have You Learned?

FOCUS: God's Gift of Peace

GOAL To review what the children have learned in Theme 4

- Go over the six questions one by one. Be sure the children are filling in the correct words. Allow time for questions or comments.
- Go over the "Words to Remember." Make sure the children can describe each in his or her own words. (Add them to your chart of "Words to Remember," if you have made one.)
- Invite the children to pray for God's guidance as they begin preparing for the actual sacrament of Reconciliation. Have them raise their arms high as they repeat after you:

Dear good and generous God,
you have filled us with your
love, joy, and peace.
We ask you, too, for
the gift of forgiveness.
Bless us as we learn how
to celebrate this sacrament of your love.
Amen.

Notes for Catechists

Communicate with Parents

At this point in the preparation process, you might want to send a note home to parents to remind them to help their child to learn an Act of Sorrow to use during the sacrament. (There is one example on page 53 of the child's book.) If they feel more comfortable with another form, such as the traditional Act of Contrition, that's fine, too. Also ask them to review with their child the Our Father, Hail Mary, Glory to God, and Sign of the Cross. If you have information about the date and time for the sacrament, or any other information that parents might need or appreciate, share it in this note as well.

5. God Gives You Forgiveness

For a few weeks, you have been learning about God's Law of Love. Now it is time to think about God's forgiveness. Let's start with a beautiful story from Jesus.

Once upon a time, there was a shepherd who had 100 sheep. He loved them very much and took good care of them. One evening, as he led the sheep back to their pen, he counted them as usual: 97, 98, 99… But where was the last one?

The worried shepherd left his other sheep and ran off to find the lost one. At last he found her at the bottom of the hill. She was stuck in a thorn bush.

Did he get mad at her? Not at all. He was so happy that he put her on his shoulders and sang to her all the way home. As he passed through the village, he invited everyone he saw to celebrate with him.

Something to Think About

- How did this story make you feel?
- Jesus calls himself the Good Shepherd. How is he like the shepherd in the story?
- What does this story say to you about God's love and forgiveness?

50

THEME: God Gives You Forgiveness

FOCUS: **Jesus the Good Shepherd searches for us when we stray.**

GOAL **To offer children immediate preparation for the sacrament of Reconciliation**

- Ask the children to focus on the illustration. What do they think is happening? Have they ever heard Jesus called "the good shepherd"? When? Read paragraph one aloud.
- Now read the story (beginning with the second paragraph) on page 50. Read it slowly and dramatically.
- Go over the "Something to Think About" question on page 50. Focus on the third question and allow time for sharing. Invite the children to study the illustration again. Does it say more to them now?

The sacrament of Reconciliation is like this story. Jesus is the shepherd who leads us to God. When we turn away from God through sin, we are like the lost sheep. When we turn our hearts once again to God, it's time for a happy **celebration**. Jesus rejoices when we stay on the path to God.

Remember that sin is something we do on purpose that turns us away from God and hurts others. Anytime we turn away from God through sin, we must find a way to turn back to God.

From the Bible

Jesus told his followers: "There is great joy in heaven when a single sinner comes back to God."
~ adapted from Luke 15:7

Let us Pray

O Lord Jesus, you are my good shepherd.
You are always with me,
so I will not be afraid.
Thank you for keeping me on the path to God.
Amen.

51

- Together, read the two paragraphs on page 51. Be sure the children understand that sin is something deliberate, something we do on purpose. Also emphasize that the good shepherd rejoices when he finds his lost sheep. In the same way, God rejoices when we try to grow in love, joy, peace, and forgiveness.
- Share the "From the Bible" words, and have the children repeat them after you. Give each child a chance to proclaim them.
- Pray the prayer together. Invite the children to fold their hands as they pray it.
- If you have time, invite the children to role-play the good shepherd story, taking turns as the shepherd and the lost sheep.

A Story of Forgiveness

Very soon you will celebrate the sacrament of Reconciliation. You will meet with a priest who will welcome you with joy. He will offer you forgiveness in Jesus' name. This story will help you understand what happens in the sacrament.

There once was a man named Zacchaeus who really wanted to see Jesus. Zacchaeus was too short to see over the crowd, so he climbed a tree. When Jesus saw him there, he said, "Zacchaeus, I think I'll come to your house for lunch today." Zacchaeus was a tax collector and the people hated him. They called him a sinner.

But Zacchaeus listened carefully to Jesus and what he said about God's Law of Love. He knew that he had taken the wrong path and had sinned. He spoke to Jesus about it because he could tell that Jesus loved him.

Jesus forgave Zacchaeus for all his sins. At the end of the meal, Zacchaeus thanked Jesus and told him how happy he was.

THEME: A Story of Forgiveness

FOCUS: **Jesus did not avoid sinners, but rather sought them out.**

GOAL **To give the children an example of the love and forgiveness Jesus showed**

- Read paragraph one. Do the children have any questions about the sacrament, such as when it will take place, who will be there, or what they will need to know? Have they memorized the prayers, especially an Act of Sorrow?
- Read the story of Zacchaeus slowly and dramatically. Have the children heard of Zacchaeus? Explain that in those days, people didn't like tax collectors because they often cheated people. The people were surprised when Jesus spoke to Zacchaeus. They thought Zacchaeus was a sinner because he cheated them. But Jesus treated him as a friend!
- Go over the illustrations and speech bubbles and invite the children to comment on them. Note that the pattern they follow is similar to what the children will experience in the sacrament. Zacchaeus confesses his sins and says he is sorry for what he did. Jesus blesses and forgives him. Highlight with the children the fact that the result is rejoicing.

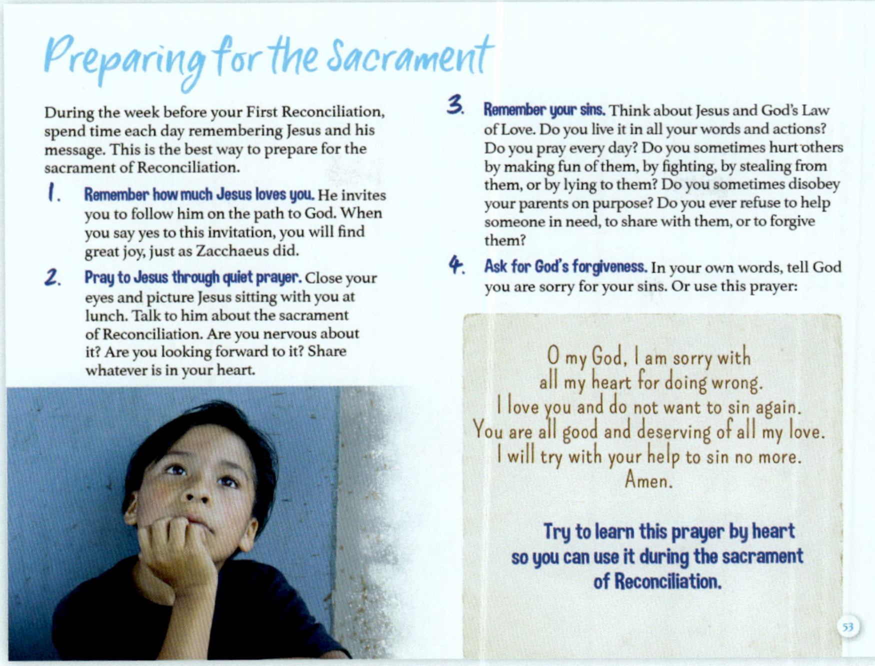

Preparing for the Sacrament

During the week before your First Reconciliation, spend time each day remembering Jesus and his message. This is the best way to prepare for the sacrament of Reconciliation.

1. **Remember how much Jesus loves you.** He invites you to follow him on the path to God. When you say yes to this invitation, you will find great joy, just as Zacchaeus did.
2. **Pray to Jesus through quiet prayer.** Close your eyes and picture Jesus sitting with you at lunch. Talk to him about the sacrament of Reconciliation. Are you nervous about it? Are you looking forward to it? Share whatever is in your heart.
3. **Remember your sins.** Think about Jesus and God's Law of Love. Do you live it in all your words and actions? Do you pray every day? Do you sometimes hurt others by making fun of them, by fighting, by stealing from them, or by lying to them? Do you sometimes disobey your parents on purpose? Do you ever refuse to help someone in need, to share with them, or to forgive them?
4. **Ask for God's forgiveness.** In your own words, tell God you are sorry for your sins. Or use this prayer:

O my God, I am sorry with
all my heart for doing wrong.
I love you and do not want to sin again.
You are all good and deserving of all my love.
I will try with your help to sin no more.
Amen.

Try to learn this prayer by heart so you can use it during the sacrament of Reconciliation.

53

THEME: *Preparing for the Sacrament*

FOCUS: **We prepare for the sacrament through prayer and reflection.**

GOAL **To help the children think and pray before celebrating First Reconciliation**

- Go over the first three points, one by one. Be sure the children understand each one. Allow time for questions.
- On point two, allow time for this brief meditative prayer. It's important to give children this opportunity to visualize "meeting" with Jesus.
- Point three is a mini examination of conscience. Be sure to point out that the children do not have to mention all their faults and failings. Instead, they can focus on something they might be doing consistently, such as making fun of classmates, not sharing, or disobeying parents.
- For point four, have them pray silently first, and then together pray the Act of Sorrow. Say each phrase aloud and have them repeat it after you.
- Remind the children that the best way to become holy and good is to spend time each day in prayer, talking to God about their day and asking for God's help. Point out the child at the bottom left of the page and ask the children to comment on what the child might be thinking.

Celebrating Reconciliation

When you meet with the priest for the sacrament of Reconciliation, you will follow a few simple steps that lead to joy and forgiveness. You do not need to remember them all. If you forget something, the priest will help you.

- First, the priest welcomes you with joy. Greet him and then make the Sign of the Cross together.
- Next, the priest will read to you from the Bible. The Bible is the book of God's Word, and a sign of God's living presence among us. God will be with you as you celebrate this sacrament.
- Now you tell the priest about times you have done wrong on purpose and hurt other people in some way. Speak to him as you would speak to Jesus. The priest will NEVER tell anyone else what you say. The priest will ask you to make up for your sins by doing a special action or saying a prayer.

THEME: Celebrating Reconciliation

FOCUS: **In this sacrament, we speak to the priest as we would speak to Jesus.**

GOAL **To give the children definite guidelines for the Rite of Penance (Reconciliation)**

- Read the first paragraph and allow the children to respond to it. Make sure they feel at ease about speaking with a priest. Some will not know the priest, so be sure to emphasize that the priest speaks for Jesus in this sacrament, and that the priest won't tell anyone what they say to him.
- Read paragraph two and practise making the Sign of the Cross together.
- Read paragraph three and show the children a copy of the Bible. Share a few examples of readings the priest might use. (Note: *In some cases, the priest might skip some of these steps, but it's best that the children are ready to listen, pray, etc., according to the rite itself.*)
- Read paragraph four. Invite the children to close their eyes and think about what fault that they would like to correct they will mention. (They are not to say this aloud to you or the class.)
- Now look at the illustrations and speech bubbles together. These are meant to assure the children that this sacrament is a time for prayer and reflection about their lives.

This is called your **penance**. It shows that you want to get back on the path to God.

- Now you tell God through the priest that you are sorry for your sins. You can use the prayer on page 53. The priest then offers you God's forgiveness with these words of **absolution**: "I absolve you from your sins in the name of the Father, and of the Son, and of the Holy Spirit." These words are the sign that God forgives you and is giving you a fresh start. At the end you answer, "Amen."
- The last step is to give thanks to God by saying a prayer of praise and sharing the greeting of peace. Then you thank the priest and leave the reconciliation room. Make sure to do or say the penance the priest has given you. Some people like to do their penance right away so they don't forget!

- Explain to the children that the "penance" the priest gives is an opportunity to follow Jesus better. Sometimes the penance is a prayer. Sometimes it is an action. Doing penance shows that we want to be followers of Jesus and want to try to make good choices from now on.
- Read the middle paragraph on page 55. Explain that the word "absolve" means to take away. In Jesus' name, the priest forgives the child's sins. The child answers, "Amen." Practise the words of absolution with each child, and have each respond accordingly. Go over the illustrations and speech bubbles so the children can picture themselves in these scenes.
- Read the final paragraph. The priest may or may not share the greeting of peace, but prepare the children for it anyway. Again, focus on the illustration on the bottom right.
- Remind the children to do the penance the priest gives them. If it is a prayer, they should pray it immediately after leaving the reconciliation room so they don't forget.

5. What Have You Learned?

Congratulations! You have made the journey to the sacrament of Reconciliation. Take a moment to think about this journey. Read page 6 in this book again.

Then think about these questions:

- What did you enjoy most on this journey?
- Was it hard sometimes? Why?
- Do you understand now how to stay close to God by living God's Law of Love?
- How did it feel to talk to the priest?
- How does it feel to have all your sins forgiven?

Now, like the children on this page, you can continue walking the path of God with Jesus. May you always enjoy God's gifts of life, love, joy, peace, and forgiveness!

Words to Remember...

Good shepherd – one who really loves and cares for the sheep. Jesus is our Good Shepherd because he cares for each one of us.

Celebration – a time to be happy and give thanks to God

Penance – a special action or prayer that shows you are truly sorry for your sins

Absolution – the words of forgiveness that the priest uses in the sacrament of Reconciliation

Let us Pray

I thank you, God of Love,
with all my heart
for all the gifts
you have given me.
With Jesus' help,
I'll walk with you always.
Amen.

56

THEME: What Have You Learned?

FOCUS: God's Gift of Forgiveness

GOAL To sum up what the children have learned, and especially to review how the sacrament is celebrated

- When newly baptized Christians have gone through the preparation process for the sacraments, they spend time afterwards reflecting on their experience. The Church calls this a time of mystagogy, a time to look back over the mysteries they have celebrated. This page serves a similar function. It invites the children to reflect on the process they have just been through.
- Ask each question and allow time for answers and comments.
- Look at the "Words to Remember." Talk about each one and be sure the children understand what the words mean. (Add them to your chart of "Words to Remember," if you have made one.)
- Pray the "Let us Pray" words aloud together. Have the children repeat them after you.
- Call each child forward. Sign each child with a cross on the forehead as you say: *"May you always walk the path of God with Jesus."* Each child answers. *"Amen."*

Order extra activities for children free of charge at twentythirdpublications.com in the FREE E-Resources section.

Thank you...

... for a job well done! You have been an important guide and mentor as the children in your care prepared for their first experience of Reconciliation. Your dedication and your willingness to share your faith are a great gift to the children, their families, and your parish.

We hope that you have grown in your faith and your understanding of Reconciliation through this rich experience. May your relationship with Jesus continue to nourish and strengthen you in all you do!

Suggestions for Your Bookshelf

Celebrating Eucharist: A Mass Book for Children. New London, CT: Twenty-Third Publications, 2011.

Clark, Connie. *My First Communion Activity Book*. New London, CT: Twenty-Third Publications, 2014.

Clark, Connie. *My First Reconciliation Activity Book*. New London, CT: Twenty-Third Publications, 2014.

Hope Dawson, Glynnis, musician John Dawson. *Guided Meditations for Catholic Kids*. Toronto, Canada: Novalis, 2018.

Lepine, Michelle. *21 Activities that Really Work*. Toronto, Canada: Novalis, 2017.

Murphy, Doris. *Learning Centers for First Reconciliation, First Eucharist, and the Whole Community*. New London, CT: Twenty-Third Publications, 2007.

Way Skinner, Christine, illustrated by Céleste Gagnon. *We Go to Mass*. Toronto, Canada: Novalis, 2017.

Way Skinner, Christine, illustrated by Céleste Gagnon. *We Pray in Many Ways*. Toronto, Canada: Novalis, 2017.

Notes

Notes

Notes

Notes

Notes

Notes